Patrick,
I hope the
Hell you ..

Steve Hosen

I Hope the Hell I Win!

Turning Hope Into Reality
...How Winners WIN!

I HOPE THE HELL I WIN!

Turning Hope Into Reality
...How Winners WIN!

Dr. Steven M. Rosenberg

Rutledge Books, Inc. Danbury, CT

Copyright© 1997 by Dr. Steven M. Rosenberg

ALL RIGHTS RESERVED
Rutledge Books, Inc.
107 Mill Plain Road, Danbury, CT 06811

Manufactured in the United States of America

Cataloging in Publication Data
Rosenberg, Dr. Steven M.
   I hope the hell I win!

   ISBN: 1-887750-69-X

   1. Self-actualization. 2. Self-culture. 3. Conduct of life.
4. Life Skills.

155.2   97-68876

Contents

Introduction vii

Preface ix

Mind Your Body

Go With It 3
    Lose Your Mind to Win Your Game

Of Plimpton, Play and Plato 13
    Philosophical Toughening — It's No Hoax: Finch May Have Been a Fink, But Philosophy Is No Fake

Be It — Meditation 21
    The Yogi Who Went Beyond Yoga - TM

Relaxation Response 31
    To Gourmet Meditation: Yoga

See It 41
    Creative Visualization and Guided Imagery

Going Under To Overcome 49
    Hypnosis and Sports

You Are What You Think 59
    The Power of Positive Thinking and Sports

Your Body's Mind

The Body Has A Mind Of Its Own 73

Beyond McDonalds and Dunkin Donuts 93
   Nutrition and Sports

What You Always Wanted to Know About Vitamins 107
   But Your Doctor was Afraid You Would Ask

Losing To Win 119
   The Need to Win over Your Own Needs

When The Cure Is Worse Than The Disease 137
   Sports Injuries and Sports Medicine

Mind, Body and Spirit

To An Athlete Living To Be Old 157

Footnotes 169

INTRODUCTION

I've had the pleasure of working with Dr. Steven Rosenberg during his association with the Philadelphia Flyers Hockey Club. On my first visit with Steve, I was skeptical that my performance as an athlete could benefit from mental conditioning. I left his office with a feeling of energy and self-confidence that I had never felt before. Since then, I have worked with Steve on relaxation, visualization, mind clearing, and other mind conditioning technics. I would like to thank Steve for helping me achieve my maximum potential as a professional athlete.

Mark Howe

PREFACE

No Shrinking

There was a call from a great boxing superstar. He wanted me to hypnotize him not to feel pain for an upcoming fight. Naturally, I refused. A guy could get killed that way. I will happily hypnotize anyone not to feel pain to go to the dentist, but not to go and get his teeth knocked out—and who knows what else?

The point is that I became a hypnotherapist because I wanted very much to help my fellow human beings. Certainly any instrument that can numb you to pain is a powerful one, and among many other things, hypnosis can help do that; and that can be extremely valuable for legitimate reasons, such as going to the dentist or for childbirth. It would be wrong in many athletic events where pain should be taken as a message to ease off or quit.

Although in my desire to help people I would not hypnotize an athlete in such a way as to desensitize him to pain, I have happily found many wonderful ways to help athletes improve their lives and their performance. Athletes have very special problems of performance, and I found myself professionally gravitating toward the world of sports because it was so challenging to work together with great athletes to overcome obstacles. And it is really a beautiful thing when you work together with another person and triumph over serious problems. It is very hard work and takes a lot of energy, but I have found it most satisfying personally.

Now, in our very complex, hightech world, life seems to have become more difficult than ever. In simpler times, it was enough to try to respond to special crises that arose, but in our times just coping has become a major crisis for millions upon millions of people. To just get out of bed and face the day is for some like having to go to battle in a terrible war. It has turned out that there are no easy answers for people with such problems from the sources of traditional medicine, psychiatry, or traditional religion and the family or educational system. What it comes down to is that to get on a right track, people need all of the help they can get. As a motivational therapist, a psychotherapist and hypnotherapist, I have found I can make some contribution, working along with others who are concerned about people.

Of course, sometimes traditional psychiatry or psychological counseling is right on, and that is, of course, very good. Other times, however, a person may require the added help of hypnotherapy, guided imagery or biofeedback. I have seen it work for people deeply troubled. I have had the opportunity to work with people whose lives were in pieces, and I really felt happy when I was able to help them get themselves well and back together.

In the course of developing material in this book, I will

have occasion to relate some of these cases in order to illustrate that we can bring the light of hope even in cases that seem hopelessly dark. Now, however, let us take our torch back to the athletic field. Here my work was exciting because it involved something really positive: how to conquer yourself in order to realize the possibility of maximum achievement or, as we say, peak performance in your field of excellence. That is a mighty goal in itself and it can be done. How to become a master in baseball, hockey, boxing or any sport is one of the most creative quests we can become involved in, but what is exciting is that we are finding that there are paths of training that lead to mastery.

We have to learn how to face those problems of becoming the consummate athlete, but now there is another thing to face. After all, the sports center doesn't exist in a vacuum. It is in the center of our troubled world, and all of the specific problems of being a superb athlete are or can be terribly complicated by the problems of life in our difficult world.

Thus, getting the athlete into shape is no simple problem. It means being able to weave and balance into harmony the psycho-physical-spiritual dimensions of reality to produce a healthy and fulfilled person who is a masterful athlete. It may *seem* impossible, but it is not. For, happily, some of those very things that will make us a better person will make us a better athlete.

I have become intensely concerned about this realization, and in this book I try to set forth important routes to self-mastery and athletic achievement. I try to show how important some working philosophy of life, a sense of meaning, meditation, visualization, hypnosis, biofeedback and nutrition can be

DR. STEVEN M. ROSENBERG

in serving the good person and good athlete.

To reinforce how vital it is to follow the right paths, I cannot help but feel pained by how often athletes seek shortcuts and get torn apart by going down the wrong paths. Just as I was in the process of preparing this preface, I was saddened but not shocked to read in the *Daily Press* that six athletes competing in the 10th Pan Am Games had tested positive for banned substances. This included American Bill Green, who had won the silver medal in the hammer throw.

This was the second consecutive drug scandal to cast a dark cloud over the Pan Am Games. Several years ago in Caracas, Venezuela, as many as thirty athletes tested positive for banned substances. This time a United States Olympic Committee spokesman stated that Bill Green's urine contained a high reading for testosterone, an anabolic steroid. Vasquez Mendose tested positive for hydrochlorthiazide, which is a diuretic. Others tested positive for beta-blockers, drugs used to decrease heart rate; for nandrolone, a steroid used to help in weightlifting; and phenylpropanolamine, a stimulant.

Whatever the accuracy of the testing in these cases, we know without question that many athletes are using steroids and chemicals to increase their performance. And that is not all. To deal with life, we know that many are hooked on dangerous drugs and alcohol. Therefore, it is urgent for the athlete to understand there is a better way. That is something I try to outline in this little volume.

In a sports column by Stan Fischler, it was pointed out that at first some hockey players viewed me as *Chewbacca* and they were leery about seeing me. They feared I might brainwash them. They also feared the stigma of being thought crazy because of going to see a "shrink." I think, however, that they have come to realize I wasn't there to *shrink* but to *expand* their sporting abilities. What I try to show in this book is that there is a road to success in sports and in life, and there are workable paths to overcoming problems, but there are no shortcuts. A king was once informed there was no royal road to geometry, and the same applies to sports. There is no royal road to athletic mastery, but I try to show there is one, if taken properly, to royal achievement.

Mind Your Body

Go With It

Lose Your Mind to Win Your Game

A small and slight Japanese man shouts, "Look at me—130 pounds—that's all!" Then he holds his arm out, as if proudly demonstrating "no muscles," and invites a hulk of a bruiser to use all of his strength to yank his arm down. The powerful big guy is smiling, radiating an air of superiority. He puts the pressure on, but the arm stays rigid. The big guy puts his all into it, but he cannot get the little guy's arm down. As if things were not embarrassing enough, the diminutive Japanese invites two other athletes with awesome musculature to join the bruiser in the task of pulling his arm down. The added power doesn't help. The arm doesn't come down. Only the pride of the three strong men comes down.

The three didn't have to worry, however, if they feared they'd lost their strength, for strength had nothing to do with the feat. In maintaining his arm against brute strength, the aikido master was not using *his* strength against his opponents, he was using *their* strength against them. If he had

I Hope the Hell I Win!

resisted with physical power or strength, his arm would have easily been pulled down. In the Japanese form of martial arts known as *aikido*, a standard demonstration is called the *Unbendable Arm*.

The key to understanding the Unbendable Arm is *ki*. Ki in Japanese is energy, and when one brings up this energy and relaxes, the arm really cannot be bent by the use of physical force. It is very beautiful, and it really works. The ki in aikido is the same type of energy the Chinese call *ch'i*, which is central to *acupuncture*. When our energy or ch'i gets out of balance, we become ill; thus acupuncture is employed to put our energy back in balance, to put us back in harmony with the universe. This is also what is achieved in the nonviolent martial art of aikido. We develop our energy and bodies to be attuned to the cosmos.

The message of aikido is valid for all sports and may help the athlete to achieve peak performance. It is beautifully expressed by Denise McCluggage in her illuminating book, *The Centered Skier*.

Look at skiers. What is the essential difference between a good skier and a poor skier? The poor skiers fight the mountain, attacking it with their tiny poles, their miniature spirits, and slashing at it with their edges. The good skiers join the mountain, commune with it, go with it. Yes, their poles stab and their edges cut, but with a difference. The difference is that the poor skiers have an I-It relationship with the mountain, to use Martin Buber's term. The mountain is a thing apart from them, an object to be manipulated and subdued. The good skiers have an I-They relation with the mountain; there is union.[1]

This is the essence for the athlete - Go With It. Get in harmony with the cosmos, and it will be natural to go with it. It doesn't matter whether it is baseball, football, tennis, golf, skiing, the martial arts, sailing, bowling, basketball, or whatever; the trick is the same: to develop your consciousness to the level that you just go with it and flow with life. In all sports, the supreme excellence is constant. It is to focus the consciousness of your whole being—mind, body, and spirit—on the activity you are engaged in so that you become one with it. You don't reflect upon it or think about it, but just naturally do it—go with it.

In Zen there is a saying: "The centipede was quite happy until a toad in fun said, Pray, which leg goes after which? This worked his mind to such a pitch, he lay distracted in a ditch, considering how to run."

In aikido, if you start thinking about what to do, it will surely be too late to do it. What is involved is the art of being completely in the spirit of whatever sporting activity you are engaged in. Then action just flows naturally; timing is perfect, and there is no need to analyze or think. You just do it.

The great Japanese athlete, Sadaharu Oh, has said that Lou Gehrig was a great inspiration for him. He explains:

Gehrig was a home-run hitter, but his greatest achievement was as "The Iron Man," playing 2,130 consecutive games. That is not just an athletic record. It is more an event of the spirit. You must be filled with something in your pressures of boredom and fatigue. There was something in him—not necessarily physical strength—that enabled him to endure. The Japanese word for spirit—power—is *ki*. Thus the *quality* of Lou Gehrig's play during his incredible stretch was as much determined by his spirit as by the "Iron" in his body. His physical body betrayed him. His spirit never did. On Independence Day, 1939, knowing that he was dying, he told fans in Yankee Stadium not only about how lucky he was but also that he was truly happy.[2]

What a fine athlete like Sadaharu Oh learns is that in sports—in baseball, as in aikido—success against an opponent depends on *timing*. He informs that you must have "the discipline to wait." And that doesn't merely mean balance. It means that the entire being has to be trained to resist the tricks and feints of a pitcher, just as one would resist an enemy holding a sword.

Put yourself in harmony with the energy flow of life. Do not step back and think, or you will fall out of harmony. Your body has its own mind, its own wisdom, and it will think for itself. Live naturally, eat naturally, and the nervous system will become reeducated.

Then, whether you are playing baseball, football, basketball, skating, or swimming, all will flow naturally, and you will *go with it*. This is what W. Timothy Gallwey means when he tells us that all games are composed of two parts—an outer game and an inner game. We have endless instructional manuals and books about how to become proficient and master the outer game. That's the game played against an external opponent to overcome an external obstacle and to reach an external goal. Gallwey, however, makes clear that this is not enough. We have got to learn the *inner* game if we want to be the best or win consistently at sports. That's what it's all about. We might say that if you don't win over yourself, you'll never win over anyone else. Gallwey explains that the inner game "takes place in the mind of the player, and it is played against such obstacles as lapses in concentration, nervousness, self-doubt and self-condemnation. In short, it is played to overcome all habits of mind which inhibit excellence in performance."³

With great insight, Gallwey reminds us that throughout the entire history of sports, the most frequent complaint of sportsmen is not that they don't know what to do, but that they don't do what they know. They break harmony with life, their unity with the game, by selfdoubt. Thus, like the centipede who was quite happy until he began to analyze what he did, they end up in a ditch. And they lose!

In *Zen of Archery*, D.T. Suzuki, the celebrated Zen master, tells us that as soon as we reflect or deliberate, we may get the arrow off the string, but unfortunately we also get off the target.

Indeed, if you want to screw up your opponent, Gallwey has helpful advice. If he is winning, merely ask him what he is doing that is making him so good that day. Get him to think about what he is doing right, and why he is doing it, and the first thing you know he will be doing it wrong. He will, in the majority of cases, become like the centipede. What we have to remember, however, is that in most cases we do this to ourselves and thus impair our game.

Tolly Burkan, who is credited with being the founder of the firewalking movement in America and is author of the book *Dying to Live*, has gotten over 100,000 people to walk over hot coals. We're talking about 1200 to 2500 degrees, sufficient to burn metal. It's absolutely amazing that people do this without injuring their feet. There have been all kinds of theories to explain how people can walk on fire, but none are acceptable, except, as Burkan, who has examined them all, tells us that the person *believes* he or she can do it. That's the whole point of it. Burkan himself tried suicide twice and suffered deep depression after having been diagnosed as having cancer. Since doctors couldn't help him, he finally reached the point at which he realized he had to help himself.

He *imaged* his cancer going away, and it did. He walked over hot coals, because he realized that if he could do that he could do many other things he had never imagined he could do in his wildest dreams. Recently in a lecture in New York, Burkan got a young lady, who had never had any martial arts training and who was not particularly strong physically, to learn to break a board with her bare hand after just a couple minutes of preparation. What was the trick? Burkan psyched her up to *believe* she could break the board, and got her to creatively have an *image* of herself doing so. And she then did it with ease.

One of the great miracles involved in firewalking is taking that first step and *believing* you can do it. If you don't take that first step and believe, it cannot happen. Strong belief can bring about electrochemical changes in the brain and thus produce the strength and energy necessary to reprogram behavior. In sports this could mean believing oneself into becoming a champion. To achieve real power, one must achieve the power of belief. Jesus, Mark 11:22-24 said:

If anyone says to this mountain, "Get up and throw yourself into the sea, with no hesitation in his heart but believing that what he says will happen, it will be done for him." I tell you therefore: everything you ask and pray for, believe that you have it already, and it will be yours.

The *belief* formula is not limited to religion but applies to

Go With It

all activities. *Believe you can do it*, and it will be yours. Research had been done and articles written to establish that it was physiologically impossible to run the mile in less than four minutes. Roger Bannister was familiar with this research, but he didn't *believe* it. In fact, he believed one could do it—could run the mile in less than four minutes. And he did it! After Bannister *showed it could be done*, the impossible was repeated 50 times. Now runners could run the mile in less than four minutes because they believed they could. In ten years' time, it had reached the point that Jim Ryan, a seventeen-year-old high school student, could run the mile in under four minutes.

Believe it with no hesitation in your heart, and you can do it. Thus firewalking, metal bending or breaking boards are accomplishments of tremendous importance for the individual. They are not merely a matter of *showing off* or sensationalism. It has been said that there is no need for a martial artist to break boards because, after all, what good is it? Nobody is ever attacked by a board. That misses the whole point. When you walk on fire, bend metal or break boards, you break the *disbelief barrier* that stands between you and accomplishment. You gain the general confidence to believe you can do things you were sure you couldn't do. Thus you race ahead to new levels of achievement. You overcome your mental obstacles, and that makes it possible to overcome physical obstacles. The same Timothy Gallwey who developed "inner game techniques" for the athlete, attended a firewalking class and claimed it improved his tennis game.

And so it is clear that being a successful athlete involves more than a beautiful body; it also involves a beautiful spirit. Charles A. Garfield, in his study of peak performance, informs us that, "some athletes said that they began to feel as though they were acting automatically, their minds and bodies like instruments perfectly tuned to the moment. They participated in the action without conscious thought." The formidable prizefighter Ingemar Johansson said that his powerful right had a *mind of its own*. People can do unbelievable things if they will only *believe*. The Olympic gold medalist Bruce Jenner commented that he felt there wasn't anything he couldn't do if he *had* to do it. If we believe and integrate body, mind and spirit, we can achieve miracles. This is what happens when we read of such feats as a grandmother lifting an automobile to save her grandchild. These stories have been checked out and often verified. In the 1940s, BenGurion used to say that despite all the unfavorable odds, he believed Israel would become an independent state, not because of the rational evidence, but because he *believed in miracles*.

Many are those who now proclaim we are on the threshold of a new age in which we will have a new way of understanding ourselves and our universe.

Of course, connected with what is hailed as the New Age are many age-old frauds, fads, follies, and superficialities; yet there are also some truly valuable breakthroughs in dealing with life. The universe is no longer understood materialistically, and a more wholesome view of life and nature is dawning. A greater respect for life, nature, women and animals than has prevailed in the past is emerging. The hope is for the creation of a more human and compassionate world.

A central area benefiting from the new wisdom is health. A *holistic* approach to health care and medicine has revealed that it is not simply a *part* of the anatomy of an organ that is sick but a *whole* person gets sick, and that manifests itself in a particular organ. Nothing in our body happens in isolation. Even if one comes down with a cold, first there is some *feeling* of being down, which has the effect of lowering the immune system. Therefore, to really cure or promote a state of health, it is necessary to deal with the whole person—to heal body, mind, and spirit.

Thus, we might use a holistic approach to sports. To really excel it is absolutely imperative to realize that sports do not merely have a physical base but that they have a philosophical ground as well. If we have a proper philosophy of life, that will encompass athletic activity and should give us the basis for doing it right. Therefore, I will discuss the importance of *philosophical toughening* as a foundation for *athletic toughening*.

In the chapters that follow, I will guide you through the types of procedures that can spell the difference between ordinary and extraordinary athletic performance for each person's capacity. Our guided tour will take us through basic material in chapters covering meditation, creative visualization, hypnosis, positive-thinking therapy, nutrition and exercise; indications of how to deal with such problems as drugs, alcohol, sleeplessness, fears, obesity and smoking; and will indicate how sports medicine can be of service. The result should be to give the athlete or any interested person a good overview of the best procedures to lead to self-fulfillment, satisfaction in living, and thus peak performance in life and sports. Some suggested exercises and procedures should help the individual immediately, but these should not be seen as a substitute for getting involved with actual sports programs or seeking guidance from professionals in the case of a true need for help

I Hope the Hell I Win!

and assistance. The book is the first step in showing the way to a new life in our new age—a better, fuller life—and thus to the best sports ability.

And now we start our journey in a chapter which looks at philosophical toughening, or proper assumptions for the good life and the sporting life.

OF PLIMPTON, PLAY AND PLATO

Philosophical Toughening —
It's No Hoax:
Finch May Have Been a Fink,
But Philosophy Is No Fake

In *Sports Illustrated* they called it "The Curious Case of Sidd Finch," and it was all very amazing: the discovery of Sidd Finch, a philosophical and mystical baseball player who zipped a 168 mph fastball. He was just great. Not only was Finch a baseball sensation, he was also a yogi, a recluse, and a devoted student of the poet-saint Lama Milaraspa. No wonder the Mets were excited about his acquisition. Perhaps one could say that Sidd Finch is the perfect pitcher, but there is one problem with saying that: He doesn't exist. It turns out that article about Finch which appeared in *Sports Illustrated* on April 1, 1985, was an April Fool's joke concocted by George Plimpton.

It was so impressive to read that Finch deflected huge

forces of the universe into throwing a baseball with bewildering accuracy and speed through the process of *siddhi* —namely, the yogic mastery of mind-body. He claimed that all acts, even throwing a baseball "are connected with the highest spiritual yearnings." What is extremely important to understand is that, while the story about Finch may have been false, it is doubtless true that all acts, including athletic feats, are indeed connected with the highest spiritual yearnings.

Philosophy literally means the "love of wisdom," and that should lead the philosopher to a fulfilling way of life. The way of life we follow affects everything we do including athletic performance. If one has a wrong philosophy, that will be reflected in the adoption of an inadequate way of life as well as in specific activities. Therefore, a successful athlete should make it a matter of great concern to operate on the grounds of a workable philosophy.

How far things can go awry with wrong philosophy can be clearly seen in the field of medicine. Contemporary Western medical practice is based to a large extent on assumptions of the French philosopher Rene Descartes. Descartes, who is often credited with being the first modern philosopher, formulated, in modern terms, the philosophy of *dualism*. According to this philosophy, *mind* or *spirit*, and *body* or the *physical* are entirely separate and distinct. The mind is spiritual substance, and the body is physical substance. The separation is fundamental for modern Western medicine. Physicians do not necessarily disbelieve there is a God or spirit, but they do in the light of their training and practice *disbelieve* God, soul or spirit has anything to do with healing the bodies of patients. They see our bodies as something purely physical, and they deal with illness on that physical level.

To modern medicine the body is only an assemblage of material parts—much as an automobile. And they are mechanics, fixing or replacing parts. They conceive of sickness in terms of a part going bad. Doctors by and large fail to come to terms with degenerative diseases that are wreaking havoc in our industrial world. This is because they are not grasping the fact that it is not an organ or a part of the anatomy that gets sick; it is a *whole person* who comes down with sickness, and that is reflected in some given part of the body. If we have a negative attitude that lowers our immune responses, we then experience sickness. To really respond to the challenge of illness, doctors must stop being high paid mechanics dealing with parts, and must start dealing with the whole person.

This same lesson applies with equal force to *sports*. We cannot look at sports or athletic performance as something purely physical. We can in our world of conflict no longer operate adequately on the assumption that the individual is divided into two: mind and body. We must understand the individual as an integrated whole. The philosophy of holism was given its first official formulation by Jan Christian Smuts, a philosopher, a general and a prime minister of South Africa. The central idea is that the furniture of the universe must be comprehended in terms of the whole or the organism rather than analyzing things into the elements or parts of which they are made.

In her book *The Holistic Revolution*, Lillian Grant proudly proclaims that all over the world a *holistic* revolution is underway and everyday gaining momentum. She says it is the "booming voice of millions." One may say that in sports this means the athlete cannot attain maximum efficiency in his or her performance by *exclusively* concentrating on the physical. The athlete requires a philosophy of life that totally harmonizes body, mind and spirit into an integrated whole. The medical doctor does not just have to defeat disease, and the athlete does not just have to defeat his or her competition, but both have to defeat the dualist philosophy of Descartes.

Dualism is the habit of the mind that divides things into two and has long been manifest in a popular stereotyping of the athlete and the intellectual. The athlete has often been understood as big, brainless and brawny, while the intellectual has been pictured as bright, but scrawny. The theme was often depicted in popular films that the strong athlete couldn't play in the big game at college because he couldn't pass his academic tests, and thus, he would have to get help from the intellectual, needless to say, a little guy. At times one would almost get the feeling that the muscular athlete didn't have a mind and the intellectual didn't have a body.

What one is coming more and more to understand is that it is not tenable to separate mind and body, and in terms of true human fulfillment one must develop mind, body and spirit as one. In the ancient world the great Greek philosopher, Plato, clearly understood that a program to develop philosophers couldn't just be mental or intellectual, but would also have to include physical training or development of the body. In his understanding, gymnastics would have to be blended and harmonized with music and intellectual training.

Actually the name Plato was not that given to our great Greek philosopher at his birth. At his birth the brilliant philosopher known as Plato was given the name Aristocles after his grandfather. The name Aristocles suggests the idea "the best will be told of him." Not long after his birth the young man was given the name *Plato*. Plato actually means *broad*, and thus one might just naturally assume that Aristocles was called Plato, meaning broad, because of his profound and broad philosophical outlook. That assumption would be wrong. He wasn't called Plato because of his broad philosophy, but because of his broad shoulders. Plato, the great philosopher, was a rugged young man in top physical condition. Plato most conscientiously practiced gymnastics and put himself through a rigorous training routine. Plato developed into so fine an athlete, that he was said to have contended for the prize of wrestling at the Isthmian festival.

It was Plato's view that simplicity in life produces bodily health, as it produces temperance in the soul. He believed an educated man should be able to manage his life physically and morally, and should have no need for doctors or law courts. As Plato understood it, physical training has to do with the soul. The two taken together should produce a harmonious development of the spirited and philosophic elements in human character. In dialogue, *Protagoras*, Plato maintained that youths are sent to the master of the gymnastic in order that the body may better minister to the virtuous mind—and further, in order that weak bodies would not let them become cowards. Finally, Plato contended that as one advances to mature intelligence, he should increase the gymnastics of his soul.

Perhaps, nowhere were the gymnastics of the soul more developed than in the ancient religion and philosophy of Hinduism. The Hindus did not merely think about the truth; they experienced and lived it. The way the Hindus discovered to bring philosophy into their lives was called Yoga. The highest form of yoga is *Raja Yoga* —it is the royal yoga. In the practice of *Raja Yoga* one learns such control of mind that as the rivers flow into and become absorbed by the great ocean, one flows into and becomes absorbed by God or the infinite. Before it is possible, however, for one to reach this elevated level of consciousness and purity, it is necessary to prepare and develop the body. Before one can ascend to the highest spiritual realization, it is necessary to perfect the physical.

This is why the study of yoga must commence with *Hatha Yoga*, which is physical yoga. Through the practice of *Hatha Yoga* one learns to coordinate mind and body to bring ultimate harmony into one's life. A basic assumption of yoga is summed up in the teaching *mens sana in corpore sano*: a sound mind in a sound body. Mind and body are not separate and distinct but a perfect unity. It is when life is understood in terms of such a philosophy that one can achieve fullest self realization. When the self is divided there is alienation, and what one does can only be done with a *part* of the self. One doesn't act efficiently because one is not acting with all of one's might. Therefore, there cannot be peak performance.

It is a fundamental teaching of Judaism and Christianity that whatsoever one does, one must do with all of his might, or with his whole heart and soul and mind. In our technological world specialization predominates and this results in psychological and sociological fragmentation. It is a widespread occurrence today that high level stress is "pulling people apart," or, as it is said, "people are going to pieces." There is need for a philosophy that will provide peace of soul and put the individual "back together."

Of Plimpton, Play and Plato

Philosophy can provide the vision of wholeness or unity that can give the individual the basis for achieving attunement to life and harmony with the world. Such a philosophical orientation when internalized can lead to peak performance in sports. For when one functions in terms of a philosophy that blossoms in a cosmic unity, there is such a sense of being a part of things that no energy is wasted. One naturally flows with and effortlessly performs at a level of optimum efficiency. In Zen it is said for all athletic activity. To grasp this philosophical ground for personal fulfillment and athletic success, it may be helpful to read *The Perennial Philosophy* of Aldous Huxley, *The Supreme Self* by Swami Abhayananda, *The Principal Upanishads*, edited by Radha Krishnan, books by Krishnamurti such as *The Only Revolution*, or *Think on These Things*, or D.T. Suzuki's *Zen Buddhism*. Immersing oneself in this philosophical orientation may in itself help one become more attuned to the rhythmic vibrations of life, and thereby help one to perform more efficiently. This should help toughen us philosophically, and philosophical toughening will translate into toughening in sports performance. When one learns to overcome the anxieties and insecurities that all people harbor about life and the universe, and develop a philosophical strength, one has a greater capacity to endure; and when one masters that, he shall master his games and play better.

Plato said there shall not be good government until philosophers are kings or until kings become philosophers. One might paraphrase and say there shall not be good athletes until athletes become philosophers or philosophers become athletes.

Of course, I do not mean at all in the technical or academic sense of being professionally a philosopher, but I do mean in the sense of having a meaningful philosophy to guide us. Victor Frankl, a great existentialist therapist, who was oppressed in a concentration camp, learned that man can endure any *how* (that is, things done to us) so long as he has a *why* (that is, meaning which is given by philosophy). One can say the athlete can deal with any *how* so long as he has a *why*.

The rest of this book will outline ways and techniques to implement a holistic and internal philosophy, and by so doing, show the way to win at your game and to deal with problems that could cause roadblocks for you. This brings us to the area of *meditation* and its value for sports.

BE IT — MEDITATION

The Yogi Who Went Beyond Yoga - TM

No matter how hot a hockey star may be, if he loses his cool he will not win his game. You can bet on that, and the bet holds true in every sport: baseball, boxing, tennis, golf, football, or basketball. If an athlete becomes stressed, tense, gets upset by too much pressure or feels nervous, his game will go off. Without being relaxed and calm, the timing will go off, and a pitcher may heave a wild ball or a boxer may throw a wild punch. Thus the good athlete not only has to be in top physical condition, but also top mental condition.

Athletes know that there is no way they can win without subjecting themselves to vigorous physical training. A careful program of physical toughening is *necessary*, but it is not *sufficient*. No matter how good the shape an athlete is in, if the mind is ill at ease or if there are worries and problems, things won't work out; the athlete won't do it! There is no question, then: any athlete who wants to do his or her best must not only go through a tough program of physical training, but also of mental and spiritual training. To be the best you can be in sports, you've got to be in condition as a whole person: body, mind, and spirit. A superb athlete must develop not only his body but his very being. This is where *meditation* comes in.

Meditation teaches the individual *inner* strength, and that can then be used to guide him or her in all outer activities. Through meditation one shuts out all external distractions and gets to the essence of things. In the highest stages of meditation one gets beyond the physical world and so elevates his or her spiritual potential so that unity with God may be realized. When one understands meditation on this high spiritual level, it may certainly seem far removed from the physical activity that must be central in sports. It is only when a person can get himself together spiritually, however, that there will be the unity of self required to most efficiently use physical energy. When one learns through meditation to shut out all distractions, one will be able to summon all of one's energy to focus completely on the athletic goal at hand.

While it is certainly true of all sports, it is most explicitly emphasized in the martial arts that there must be a coordination and unity of mind and body that can be realized through meditation. Susan Ribner and Dr. Richard Chin tell us that what is common to all of the martial arts is that "they are a means for developing physically, mentally and spiritually, and not just a fighting method for defeating one's enemies."[1] They further point out, speaking of the Shaolin fighters (those who first developed martial arts), that "they spent their days in meditation . . . seeking perfection of character."

Be It — Meditation

Taisen Deshimaru explains, "through *zazen*, an unadorned form of sitting meditation, the samurai could effectively still the restless mind, perceive the ultimate harmony beneath seeming discord, and achieve the oneness of intuition and action so necessary for *Kenjutsu* (sword fighting).[2] The student of martial arts who properly disciplines himself so harmonizes his body, mind and spirit that full power is concentrated in his being to render him the most potent fighting force. Taisen Deshimaru comments, "To practice Zen or the martial arts, you must live intensely, wholeheartedly, without reserve—as if you might die in the next instant."[3] This advice would apply equally to every sport—live wholeheartedly and put your whole self into what you do, and you will give the very best. As it is observed in the book *The Wisdom of Bruce Lee*, "such power cannot be learned by hours of weight-lifting or routine drills in a gymnasium."[4] The authors, Felix Dennis and Roger Hutchinson, say that the power must have a spiritual source and be attained by meditation and lengthy reflection.

It is through meditation that you learn to *become* what you *do*, and that is power! *Techniques* develop our athletic skills, but meditation develops our *being*, and that provides us with the will and resolve to perfect the skills. Deshimaru says, "Zen and the martial arts are not things that you *learn* or do. They are what you *are*."[5]

Yogis, Zen masters and *sifus* (chinese teachers of martial arts) devote themselves, and spend long hours in meditation each day. This may not seem practical for the busy athlete in our world of timetables and schedules. I recall advising a harried executive, who was plagued by painful headaches and tension as a result of his stressful work, that he should meditate each day. He seemed disturbed, and snapped: that would be fine for someone who had time, but he certainly did not. A couple of months later he suffered a nervous breakdown, and had to be away from his work for a lengthy period.

Not only does meditation not *waste* time for us, but by helping us to relax and rid ourselves of tension, it makes possible the most efficient and effective use of our energy; therefore, we actually save time, and often ourselves. Nonetheless, people may find it impossible to set aside lengthy periods each day to meditate. Thus, it is fortunate that programs of meditation have been set up that are based upon economical time schedules. One of the best known and effective of these is *Transcendental Meditation,* also known as *TM.* This certainly has great value for the athlete.

In a world of high-tech living, characterized by constant change, speed, conflict, division, fragmentation and disharmony, meditation provides relief by taking us deep within, where one may find peacefulness, harmony and unity. In our industrialized world of mass production and mass consumption the self tends to get lost in the turbulent sea of external stimuli which constantly bombards us.

Meditation, by leading us beyond this, can return us to the self and the strength that brings. When a power line becomes overloaded, it blows out. When the nervous system becomes too overloaded with a barrage of stimuli, it too blows out, and the individual snaps. The great welter of activity pulls us off center, and we suffer a personal energy crisis. Meditation comes from a word which signifies getting to the center. Meditation returns us to the center of ourselves, and thus enables us to summon energy needed to deal with our challenges. Meditation is a means of shutting off the interference of outer stimuli, of focusing us inward where the mind becomes still and leads us beyond stress and pressure. Therefore meditation is not a way of avoiding life, as some try to criticize, but a way of providing us with the energy to come to terms with life, and certainly to achieve peak performance in such activities as sporting events.

For the harried businessman or athlete, Transcendental Meditation may be just what is needed for more energy and tranquility. Transcendental Meditation, or TM, was brought here by Maharishi (meaning great seer) Mahesh Yogi. He first came here in 1959 and his ideas spread like wildfire all over the planet. What makes this method, which can produce deep relaxation, so appealing is that it can be learned in an hour or two, and only need be practiced for two 15 or 20 minute periods each day.

Maharishi sought to bring the individual to the very center of the self by combining the ancient spiritual tradition of Hinduism with modern Western science. What he did was to tailor ancient wisdom and methods to the modern world and in a means open to scientific evaluation. He himself was a disciple of a great wise man, Guru Dev. When Guru Dev passed on in 1953, Maharishi retired to the Himalayas where he serenely maintained himself in a cave. During this time he felt something calling him back to the world. The urge he experienced was a mission to bring the wisdom of ancient India to those suffering in the modern world.

What Maharishi taught is very simple and easy to learn, and yet it works. Instead of retiring from the world for long periods of meditation according to this teaching, it is only necessary to meditate twice a day for periods of 15 or 20 minutes each. While not necessary, it is best to sit in a quiet and comfortable place. Then one will close the eyes, and simply let the mind flow freely. This separates TM from most systems of meditation which emphasize *concentration* or *control*. Maharishi insisted that those who emphasized deep concentration or mind control failed to understand the nature of the mind. They did not realize that the mind in *wandering* wasn't simply moving about aimlessly, but was searching for fulfillment. This is exceedingly important. People sometimes get uptight in working against the wandering. That defeats the purpose.

In TM, on the contrary, we simply go with the wandering. Maharishi explains that it is the nature of the mind to move onto a field of greater happiness. Actually *concentrating* on something in particular may lock the mind at one level, and thus prevent it from moving to the deepest levels of consciousness. There should not be any analysis, contemplation or concentration. Thus, one does not have to believe in any religion or philosophy to do transcendental meditating. Maharishi likens it to diving into a pool of water. The diver simply has to let go, and nature's laws will take care of the rest. All one has to do, then, is let the mind go, and it will seek fuller happiness.

As one lets the mind flow, it is necessary to repeat a very special sound over and over to oneself. This sound is called *mantra*. It is important to emphasize the *mantra* is a *sound*, not a word. A word has meaning, and that would cause us to think about the meaning, and to become distracted. A sound, on the other hand, is not going to our mind for analysis, but has a direct effect on our nervous system. A sound wave is a physical reality in its own right, and can move us in a variety of ways. Thus, at the very outset, an instructor in TM selects a special sound, a mantra for the beginning student. The sound quality will then click in the being of the students and produce peace and elevated consciousness.

One of the most basic mantras is *OM,* a sacred sound in India, which when meditated upon should lead to feelings of cosmic unity. Of course, an instructor in TM recognizes each individual is unique, and an important part of TM is to select a mantra that fits the needs of the particular individual.

If in letting the mind flow one starts *thinking* about things, it is necessary to simply return to the mantra. One should not strain, but rather seek to go slowly, easily and naturally. When the meditation comes to an end, in about 20 minutes, there must not be any abrupt return to the world. One should sit quietly for about three minutes and open the eyes slowly. This will avoid any shock to one and bring about a natural transition.

Transcendental Meditation is really simple, and it works. Meditation has been studied in carefully controlled laboratory settings. Dr. Robert Keith Wallace and Dr. Herbert Benson of Harvard Medical School undertook a comprehensive study of TM. Wallace and Benson discovered in all of the meditators an immediate reduction of oxygen consumption of 16-18 percent. A comparable reduction in oxygen consumption was not discovered under hypnosis. The decrease in oxygen was found to be accompanied by a decrease in carbon dioxide metabolism. The reduction in oxygen consumption and carbon dioxide metabolism shows that one's physical system is relaxed and operating naturally. This reveals the system is slowing down and realizing tranquility.

Supporting evidence was also provided by observation of galvanic skin response (GSR). GSR measures resistance of the surface of skin to an electric current. Increased GSR shows there is decreased anxiety. When one can get into a relaxation state and become free of tension, GSR increases. Thus in deep relaxed sleep GSR increases about 200 percent. In TM some individuals actually had a 500 percent increase of GSR.

People suffering from anxiety neurosis or high blood pressure experience an *increase* in blood lactate. Transcendental meditators underwent a *decrease* in blood lactate. Another finding that should be of interest to athletes was that mediators revealed a faster reaction time as well as speedy recovery to the shock of a sudden stimulus.

I believe I can say without qualification that there is much benefit to be derived from a program such as TM. I have tried to put it in a nutshell: sit in a quiet and comfortable place for two periods of 15 to 20 minutes daily. Close your eyes, let your mind flow freely, and repeat a mantra. One should enter the gates of a blissful state. When the time is up, come out gradually and back to activity with increased vigor. While at first one will find his or her own place to meditate, later one will develop the knack of being able to meditate in any place—on a crowded bus, plane or train!

Can one undertake this program of meditation on his or her own, or is it necessary to seek instruction from qualified teachers?

TM people insist that one cannot go it alone and must have their guidance—and they must have your money. Of course, it is always wise and fortunate to have a reliable guide to help you meditate properly. There are TM centers all about, and millions of people have benefited from professional instruction. If, however, one is cautious and realistic, it is possible one can do it on his or her own. One should be patient, willing to stick with it, and not expect instant success.

One of the primary services rendered by TM instructors is to carefully choose a *mantra* for the student. This does, indeed, provide valuable assistance. Again, however, while it may be better to receive your special sound from qualified TM teachers, it is not impossible to choose your own. Thus, keeping in mind the fact that you would be better served to have an instructor work out a personal mantra for you, we will herein list some sounds that may serve as mantras, and what you must do is look them over and see if one of them seems to fit your personality.

THE MANTRAS:

OM	SHANTI
OM SHANTI	AUM
JAYA GANESHA	HARI OM
KRISHNA	OM KALI
HARO HARA	NARAYAN
RAM	RAMA
SHIVO HAM	OM SO HAM
NAMAH	MANGALAM
NAMO	RAMA NAMA
HARI RAMA	HARI KRISHNA
MAHA	SRI MAHA
SHIVAYA	OM NAMAH SHIVAYA
SITA	BIJA

THE MANTRAS (continued)

Sita Ram	Om Tat Sat
Atma	Ayam
Sarvam Eva Braham	Om Mani Padme Hum
Tan Mam Avatu	Dum
Gam	Yam
Ham	Lomaku
Salaba	Ang
Bilaji	Talayi
Suaha	Targ Tutare
	Ture Swaha
Shabda	Tam

If you are able to successfully do TM on your own, that is well and good. If you experience difficulties, do not worry. Perhaps, if that happens, it would be well to seek qualified help from a TM center. If this doesn't appeal, you should know there is another "do it yourself" westernized version. To that we now come.

RELAXATION RESPONSE
To Gourmet Meditation: Yoga

In our mass age, when it has become commonplace to make complicated things simple, Maharishi has made meditation simple, but not so simple that one could do it without the help of his people. That is, one can do it, not alone. Now, enter Dr. Herbert Benson. He outdid TM by presenting a "Do it Yourself" program of meditation. In the ceremony of meditation Maharishi had the boldness to cut down the time. Along came Benson, and cut out the ceremony.

In TM one goes through introductory lectures, interviews, follow-up sessions, regular checking, meetings (optional), and receives newsletters. Upon arriving for personal instruction, the new student is asked to bring flowers, a white handkerchief and fruit, goes through a ceremony given in the Sanskrit language, and receives the special sound or mantra. It is not much, and one, of course, doesn't give allegiance to any religion or philosophy. It is simply the providing of some atmosphere. No atmosphere is required in Benson's *relaxation method*. Benson's method gets directly to the essence, and eliminates all embellishment.

Here's all there is to *relaxation response*: The individual has to go to a quiet and comfortable place. The next step is just to sit still in a relaxed position, close the eyes, and go through the procedure of relaxing all muscles in the body from head to foot. The next step is to breathe through the nose, become aware of the rhythm of the breathing, and then breathe out and while doing so silently utter the word "One." *Inhale*, and say nothing, and then *exhale* repeating the word, " One." It is important not to force it but to breathe naturally and easily. This process of natural breathing through the nose while saying "One" when exhaling should be practiced for 10 to 20 minutes, twice daily, two hours before or after eating so as not to affect digestion and thus interfere with relaxation. As in TM, when the period of meditation ends, it is important to come out of it slowly. Open the eyes gradually, and do not stand up immediately.

The relaxation response method proves to be as effective against stress, tension, hypertension, high blood pressure and frustration as TM. Scientific study of the *relaxation response* established that it was effective in reducing the frequency of abnormal heartbeats. These are known as PVC's or premature ventricular contractions. If the heart beats too rapidly, it may not pump enough blood through your body. Of course, it cannot be overemphasized that any beneficial results of TM or relaxation response should never be substituted in the case of any medical problems for professional help.

The big difference between TM and relaxation response lies

in the fact that in Benson's technique no specific *mantra* is employed—although one may say that the "One" which the meditator repeats serves as a mantra. Also, of course, whereas there is a conscious breathing rhythm in relaxation response, there is none in TM. TM defenders insist that any concentration, even on the breath, is unnatural and thus impedes the natural flow of the mind. On the other hand, it may be contended that proper rhythm of the breath can connect now with the rhythm of life. Of course, for the TM meditator the mantra serves this purpose. Which approach is best? Both. Whichever suits the particular individual should be chosen by that individual. Some people will find that the mantra and natural flowing of the mind will produce optimum health and positive feeling; for others, concentration upon breathing while saying "One" will be just what the "doctor ordered," as the saying goes. The point is that there are many paths to enlightenment, and what may work for one person may not for the other. Some may even find it is more fulfilling to practice what we may say is the gourmet of meditation, or *yoga*.

To begin the practice of yoga marks a turning point in one's life, because *doing* yoga transforms one, and brings on a new life, a more healthy, peaceful and fulfilling one. There are various types of yoga, and the one people usually begin with, and which would certainly be highly beneficial to the athlete is *Hatha Yoga*. Hatha Yoga results in mastery over our bodies and thus prepares us for spiritual mastery.

Yoga meditations have been practiced from time immemorial in India, but it was not until about 200 B.C. that a great teacher named Patanjali appeared and put together the first systematic organization of the basic principles of yoga. This formalization of yoga practices is provided in Patanjali's book called *Yoga Sutras*. The *Yoga Sutras* taught us the correct path to moral and physical well-being, proper programs of exercise, concentration, meditation, psychic powers and spiritual liberation. There is no question that following such a program would contribute enormously to the making of the well-rounded athlete, capable of peak performance.

The basic goal of yoga is to make the mind *still* in order that one might become aware of the true self. When one learns that his or her essence is in perfect tune with the universe, one becomes free. The way to achievement of this is to be found through specific steps, known as the "limbs of yoga." These include a *moral* phase, involving that which the individual should abstain from, positive duties, or practices to be undertaken; a *physical phase*, involving *postures*, or a program of conditioning of the body and nervous system; and *breath control*, consisting of fundamental breathing exercises, concentration, meditation, and ultimately absorption in the infinite.

The program may not sound appealing to the athlete, but believe or not, in the long run, it`s better than steroids.

In yoga it is understood that one should start one's journey toward self-realization and spiritual perfection by developing moral purity. It is important to live by an ethical code of high standards. This is certainly central to good sportsmanship; and lacking it, the athlete fails in his obligations to himself and his fellow athletes.

According to yoga, the individual *should not* be sexually over indulgent, be greedy, lie, or steal. There are also *positive* observances. One *should* be pure, austere, contented, read sacred scriptures, and be devoted. These may seem excessive, and far removed from sports, but to lead the good life should help get one more in harmony with reality, and thus have less hang-ups on the playing field or in the arena. Usually when there is a moral breakdown, a physical breakdown follows. Thus, to follow practices that keep the individual straight has implications for athletics.

After one learns to follow a moral code, it is important to get the body into condition. This is achieved in yoga through what are called the *asanas,* or the *postures.* If one has a poor posture, performance will also be poor. Any posture may be comfortable, but must be firm. Yogic postures enable the individual to remain in a fixed pose for an extended period of time, and thus enhance powers of concentration, meditation and optimum use of energy.

Of the many yogic postures some of the classic ones are the headstand, the savasana, the Lotus pose, the Cobra pose, or squatting pose. In the *savasana,* or so-called Death Pose, one must lie flat and heavy on the mat. The point is to feel the weight of the body pushing to the ground. Next, every single muscle in the body must be relaxed, going from head to toes. This asana will bring the most thoroughgoing release of tension, and the realization of a relaxed state. Perhaps the most famous posture is the *Lotus Pose.* This is the position in which one sits tailor fashion with legs crossed and spine always straight.

All of the many postures practiced in yoga, which may readily be found and illustrated in hundreds of introductory books published on yoga—or mastered in beginning courses, which are given almost everywhere—help the individual to develop control over the body and its mechanisms. Yoga loosens us up, rejuvenates us and promotes a sense of peacefulness.

If any of us, however, in the Western world fail to find yogic postures natural and easy to assume, it is in that case better not to force. Instead, a firm, comfortable and erect position that is natural should be assumed, At this point it is time for breathing exercises, and then on to concentration and meditation.

Absolutely essential as a complement to the asanas, or postures, are the breathing exercises, known as *Pranayama*. Pranayama, or correct breathing, is viewed as the link between the physical and the spiritual. Americans are the greatest people in the world for developing "know how," and yet, ironically, most of us do not know how to breathe properly. It goes without saying: correct breathing for the athlete is *vital*. It will be basic in bringing the energy necessary *to do it*.

Too many people breathe in through the mouth. It's not a good idea to put your foot in your mouth when you talk, and it is not a good idea to put air in the mouth when you inhale. The correct manner of breathing is with the mouth closed, and with air taken in through the nasal passages; in that manner, the air inhaled is properly filtered by the mucous membranes in the nose. Another " *no, no*" is *rapid* breathing. If breath is short and fast, the mind will be negatively affected. Such a breathing pattern will cause nervousness. Breathing should be in a rhythmic pattern. First, there must be inhalation through the nose, and very importantly, retention before exhalation. As a simple starting point, breathe in deeply for a period of about two seconds, hold the breath for four seconds, and then breathe out slowly for four seconds.

RELAXATION RESPONSE

There are, of course, a variety of breathing techniques, but there is a common element, and it is that in all cases the student learns to control erratic and restless activity of the mind in order to be prepared for concentration and activity involving expenditure of energy.

Circulation of the blood in the lungs is maintained by the beating of the heart, and this vital activity is facilitated by the movements of inhalation and exhalation. The very best athletes can reach peak performance without altering heart and breathing rhythms. This means they have had to live in such a way that a life in harmony with nature and physical training have programmed the heart and lungs to do more work without a higher consumption of energy. Slow, harmonious, rhythmic breathing promotes the mental faculties and relaxes the mind. When the mind is troubled, the heart speeds up, the pulse quickens, breathing is difficult, and the athlete's performance is sabotaged. Thus, yoga can play a most important role in keeping the athlete in harmony with life.

There can never be complete mastery of the body while the mind is not disciplined. If the mind is easily distracted, one will not be able to focus the energy essential to the most efficient use of the body. It is very clear that if a person cannot control himself, then someone else will control him, body and soul. In sports competition that would translate into losing. Therefore, it is imperative one be in control of one's own mind.

It is easy to demonstrate how difficult a task it may be simply to get in control of one's mind. Take a fountain pen, a ballpoint pen, a pencil or any simple object, and focus your concentration on it *exclusively* for one minute without thinking of anything else. In most cases people will find they cannot hold pure concentration on that one object for more than a few seconds, after which time their minds will *wander*. What this means is that we cannot do with our minds what we wish to. We are not in charge of our own minds. We cannot protect or guard our own minds from thoughts or ideas we do not want to intrude. Of course, if we cannot be in charge of our own mind, we will not completely be in charge of our body. This is why the higher step in yoga, *concentration* is so important. It develops in us the ability to control our minds.

In the effort to develop powers of concentration in order to gain control of one's own mind, one might do well to start with a simple concrete object such as a pen. Try to focus exclusive attention on it for a short period of time, gaze at it, and direct all thoughts to it. If you find your mind wandering, do not become angry or upset, but calmly return your attention to the pen, or whatever object you have chosen. The point is not to do this perfectly as you start, but to have *determination*. Stay with it, and eventually you will develop the mind power you seek.

In order to strengthen concentration, a fine exercise is to gaze at a point or small object without blinking for a short period. It is helpful to look at the point of one's nose. If the eyes are not strained this will contribute toward strengthening them. Doubtless one of the most valuable exercises involves focusing the eyes on a lighted candle. This exercise is best carried out in a dark room. Focus the eyes upon the lighted candle and hold them steadfastly. Do so for a couple of minutes. Upon finishing the act of gazing at the lighted candle, if the hands are cupped and placed over the eyes, it will then be possible to concentrate upon the afterimage of the lighted candle.

We may train concentration not only with the eyes but with the ears. This may be achieved simply by attending our hearing to the ticking sound of a clock, or even a watch, in an otherwise quiet room. Another helpful method consists of *concentration* upon our own breathing pattern. One may also count each inhalation. All of this will have a soothing effect upon the mind, and assist us in the task of taking charge of ourselves in order that we may direct our energy as we wish and achieve our tasks.

In the practice of yoga one graduates from concentration to *meditation*. In meditation all of one's energy is centered on one thing. Meditation is derived from a word which means getting one back to the center—to the center of oneself. Thus in meditation one focuses on the center of the inner self and all else is blocked out. The value of this for the athlete is limitless. In any athletic contest, if the athlete doesn't have his or her energy unified, there is division, and all cannot be given to the athletic event or competition. Thus, if meditation is a withdrawing from the world, it is to give the strength and unity to return to the world with maximum effectiveness.

We require the stillness of mind and unity of energy meditation results in to give our best, and to really achieve a particular goal we are well-served by another mental exercise called *imaging*. Picture what you want, *and you can do it*.

We now come to the chapter on imaging.

SEE IT

Creative Visualization and Guided Imagery

The statement "seeing is believing" is a skeptical utterance, meaning "I will only believe something if I actually see it happen." There is another way one can understand the statement "seeing is believing." It is that even though something actually *didn't* happen, or is highly unlikely to happen, if one can *visualize* it or see it in his or her mind, then it will happen. If you really want something to happen, get a clear picture of it in your mind, because chances are *seeing it* will bring it into being.

Some people in the medical profession are now relying upon visualization to heal patients. If a cancer patient can get a clear picture in his mind of a white blood cell attacking a malignant tumor, he can recover. Anyone who can get a clear image in the mind of something he or she wants, can make it *happen*. This really works in all aspects of life, and I can personally testify that it works in sports, for as a motivational therapist for the Philadelphia Flyers I have seen it work. If the hockey player can *visualize* a winning performance, then, when he gets out on the ice, he will make it happen.

When the great hockey star Pelle Lindbergh lost his life in a senseless automobile accident, I was terribly shaken. The two of us had become close friends. He had even had me visit him at his home in beautiful Sweden. I had the honor of working hard together with Pelle to help him perform at a peak level. I am not trying to take personal credit for his success as a hockey player for the Flyers, but am only recalling my work with him, which leaves me with so many sad associations, and giving credit to this method of *visualization*.

Although the tragedy struck that bleak November day back in 1985, it still hurts as if it were only yesterday. Nonetheless, painful though it may still be to remember, remember one must, certainly in respect of the important contribution Pelle Lindbergh made to the game of hockey and to the use of visualization to realize *peak performance*. This contribution and what we do in visualization was nowhere more aptly expressed than in an article by a fine writer, Ray Didinger. Here is what he had to say:

> The night Pelle Lindbergh received the Vezina Trophy, he publicly thanked two men. One was Bernie Parent, his tutor and role model.
>
> The other was I, Dr. Steven M. Rosenberg. I didn't know how to react. I was embarrassed and flattered at the same time. That was typical of Pelle, though, he was always giving other people credit.

See It

> I suppose it all sounded very mysterious, the goal tender and the psychotherapist...but there was no hocus-pocus. Mostly Pelle and I just talked.[1]

In *guided imagery* or, as it is also called, *programmed visualization*, I can guide athletes to create positive pictures in their minds which will then be acted out in their sporting endeavors. Adelaide Bry, a counseling psychologist and a business consultant on communication problems, makes an observation that is very much verified in my own practice. It is as follows:

> By visualizing very precisely whatever changes we want and then seeing our life as we want it to be, we can heal our bodies, have our dream house, get the job we want, improve a relationship with someone we love, and even win a championship sports even.[2]

We all know an athlete cannot go into any sporting event without having trained long and hard, but if the athlete wants not merely to compete but to give it his or her best, then any program of training should be complemented with the practice of visualization. Harold Sherman tells us, "I found that if I pictured in my mind what I wanted to accomplish, before I acted, that I was much more effective in every physical movement I made. Today this power of visualization is widely used and being taught by instructors in different sports."[3]

In playing basketball Sherman took a snapshot picture in his mind of the loop it would require to hit the basket from wherever he was on the floor, and, alas, then his muscles propelled it in just the right arch, and in it went. Sherman also used *visualization* with much success in baseball. When he had to pitch, he would take mental aim at the mitt, and as long as he could maintain his concentration the ball would go to the visualized object.

Harold Sherman also relates visualization to sports he did not engage in such as football or golf. Of football he says, "Each member of a football team has to carry the image in his mind of the part he is trained to play in whatever position he is assigned. He must see an instant picture of each play as it is called and what he is supposed to do when the play is executed."[4]

As for golf, athlete Jack Scott, who is a friend of Harold Sherman, teaches what he calls "Visual Golf" in Arizona. Jack Scott began to "picture" what he wanted some years ago as a result of reading books of Sherman's. Now many leading golfers are using visualization. The golfer surveys each lie before each stroke, *pictures* which club to use, how hard to hit the golf ball, and gets an image in the mind of just where it is wanted to land or how far to roll.

Visualization has a most important role to play in athletic training; and it is not really difficult. One must created an image or picture in one's own subconscious mind, and hold on to it until it becomes reality. How does one go about creating this image? That is, what are the best mechanics?

It is important to commence any visualization program by becoming relaxed. This may well begin by sitting quietly and consciously breathing. As we have said previously, breathe in slowly through the nostrils, hold that breath as long as possible, and then exhale slowly through the mouth.

SEE IT

Next, eyes should be closed, and an effort should be made to keep your mind blank. To assist in the effort to empty the mind, opening the eyes after a restful period and staring at a small bright object may help. This will help clear the mind of distractions.

When there is a feeling of *relaxation* and the mind is *blank*, it is helpful to imagine seeing an empty movie screen. Visualize on the screen, and put your objective on the screen. Always have faith and believe that what you have visualized will happen. Of course, there are many methods that may properly be followed to develop in us the skill to visualize. We have only given one, but one can use the imagination to proceed in a way most suited to his or her needs.

One thing is certain. It is that if we do develop our powers of visualization, as Andrew Wiehl states in his book *Creative Visualization*, "Many wonderful things will begin to happen. Doors will open for you, people will turn to you, and opportunities will present themselves."[5]

Now some people may fear doors will not open for them, because they are incapable of *imaging*, because they cannot actually see images in front of their eyes. These people must be assured that inner imagery can be achieved on the audio or kinesthetic as well as visual level. In other words, while some people may *vividly* see pictures, others may instead hear *audible* sounds, while still others may *feel* images in their bodies. There are, of course, also those who will combine different senses. For example, they may *taste* and *smell*.

One approach is to get a list of words, shut your eyes, and then listen to those words. Try to *see* a picture in the mind associated with those words, or try to *hear* a sound, or try to *feel* the words in your body, and then smell or taste the words. You might take one word, let us say "snow," and first try to see it, and then feel it, and so on, and after that try to experience the word with many senses all at once.

This type of practice will help to more completely experience images and to receive more information concerning them. If you are experiencing problems *imaging*, one exercise many professionals use involves the act of shutting your eyes, and then *seeing* yourself biting into a sour lemon, or a spicy hot pepper. If it's a lemon, *feel* how sour it tastes in your mouth. Feel it in your throat, perhaps on your teeth.

With a little practice most people can become adept at imaging, and as a result of this will be able to *do it* at the important sporting event. I get my athletes to "fine tune" their minds and deeply relax. I personally refer to their visualization exercises as *positive day dreaming*. The athletes must *visualize* that they are actually out there on the ice doing everything they are supposed to be doing. I get them to practice in their minds that they are there in the Stanley Cup finals. This procedure builds motivation and confidence, and they *can do it*: get out their and do their best.

Mark Howe, the Norris Trophy candidate, was my first patient. He had been referred to me by Pat Croce, at that time, the Flyers conditioning coach. Mark had sustained an injury, and the coach was concerned to make sure it wouldn't produce any mental flak when he got back to playing. The goal was to bring him back, and have him come in with full strength. He went right out and scored. Mark and I had many sessions, and he kindly believed it did put new life and rejuvenation into his career.

SEE IT

"Steve, Thanks for (the) tremendous help you gave me as a player and for making me a very happy person. Your friend Mark Howe"

I think it is fair to say that in working with hockey players and athletes in other areas, there have been very concrete results. It is not due to any magic, however. It simply requires practicing the methods of visualization, and whatever sport the athlete happens to be in doesn't matter. There should be positive results. The game should be improved. Of course, nothing occurs in a vacuum. We have discussed the value of practicing techniques of meditation and concentration, and they can certainly be combined with visualization to contribute to peak performance. Another method, I, as a professional hypnotherapist, can personally testify to as having significant results is hypnosis. Combined with visualization, hypnosis can be a powerful weapon in the athletic arsenal as a beneficial procedure for the achieving athlete. *Meditation* can get us to *be* one with our activity, and thus maximize our energy; *visualization* can get us to actually *see* us achieving our goals, and thus build necessary confidence; *hypnosis* should remove any blocks we may have, and thus really free us to actually *do* it. This, of course, brings us to our discussion of hypnosis.

GOING UNDER TO OVERCOME

Hypnosis and Sports

In March of 1951, in the beautiful city of Copenhagen, all hell broke lose when a man named Hardrup robbed a bank, and shot and killed two employees. He received two years in a mental institute for that nefarious deed. A man named Nielsen, however, was given the maximum sentence of life in prison and he wasn't even at the scene of the crime. How could this be? It so happened that Nielsen *hypnotized* Hardrup to commit the crime.

Dr. Paul J. Reiter, one of Denmark's most eminent psychiatrists and a distinguished authority on hypnosis, testified that Hardrup was *controlled* by *hypnosis*. Shades of Svengali! There does exist a widespread fear that unscrupulous hypnotists can take away a person's will and induce him to do terrible things. There is a tendency for people to think of hypnosis in Hollywood terms. John Barrymore as the diabolical Svengali, in the film version of du Maurier's novel, became obsessed with the lovely young Trilby, and put her under his hypnotic spell. It was all very effective, and with a few Bela Lugosis, as a mad hypnotist thrown in Hollywood films, it was easy for people to get the idea that hypnotists were evil geniuses. It is important to understand that this is very far from the truth. Hypnotists cannot get subjects to do things against their will or moral code, and the majority are there to help people solve problems.

The hypnotist is not there to put anyone under a spell and induce him to engage in negative acts. On the contrary, the hypnotist can be a very positive force to *free* individuals from bad habits or negative behavior patterns, and help them become more positive. Indeed, hypnotism can do wonders with athletes. I myself have had excellent results in employing hypnosis in connection with athletes, and I am not alone in that regard.

The onetime light heavyweight boxing champion Melio Bettina found that hypnosis assisted him in an impressive boxing career. It is now agreed his pugilistic abilities were underrated. His manager, James Vi Grippo, was a hypnotist and put Melio under hypnosis with unsuccessful results. Bettina fought Billy Conn, and got beaten. Then he had a rematch and got whipped again. If you are fighting a Billy Conn you don't need hypnosis to put you under—his fists can do it! The handsome boxing star Lou Nova practiced yoga, and that greatly helped him in his boxing. He even did the yoga posture of standing on his head—excellent for the circulation. Then he fought Joe Louis, and was left laying on his back. Fighting Joe Louis is not good for the circulation.[1]

It is very important to understand something. Hypnosis can help you be the *very best* you can be, and if the *potential* is buried in you to be a champion, *hypnosis* can bring it out, and that makes it a wonderful tool for the athlete. If it is not in you, however, to become a great concert pianist or to knock out Joe Louis, hypnosis is not going to work a miracle. It will, however, get you to do your best, and that is good enough. Here is an example: The hypnotist Dr. David F. Tracy worked with the St. Francis College basketball team. They were doing poorly, and were given very little chance in the Catholic League Tournament, but after Dr. Tracy worked with them and taught them to release nervous tension and relax through hypnosis they almost won.

Many athletes get nervous and lose confidence. Ballplayers have struck out because of that. In baseball Dr. Tracy worked with the St. Louis Browns, and through hypnosis planted the suggestion that the player would be confident and relaxed. Pitchers in particular would tighten up due to nervousness, and thus pitch wild balls. What a good hypnotist can do is get the pitcher to form an image in his mind of just where he wants the ball to go, relax, and then *freed* of tension, *do it*, throw the ball to the right place.

I have been eminently satisfied with the results of hypnosis in conjunction with hockey players. Others have as well. Dr. Tracy helped the New York Rangers hockey team. Back in 1951 they fell into a serious losing streak. By the third period in every game, everyone on the team had become exhausted. They would sacrifice a lead they had built up and lose in the last period. Through hypnosis Dr. Tracy got the players to relax and restored confidence. After that the team made a great comeback.[2]

Hypnologist Sidney Petrie comments, "The St. Louis

Browns sought the assistance of a hypnologist to raise their sagging batting average more than twenty years ago. Since then hypnotic conditioning has been used successfully by basketball players, both amateur and professional in a long list of sports."[3] Petrie notes there are dramatic reports of new endurance, new speeds, and new records.

Players mess up their games in golf or bowling by feeling the pressure of needing to attain a certain score or win. Tension and anxiety develop. Then one's natural abilities get turned off. Through hypnosis the natural harmony, rhythm, timing, and confidence to win can be turned on. Hypnosis can take away strain, and thus put one back in the groove. One doesn't get hung up on the small details of his performance, but, feeling relaxed and confident, just naturally connects and achieves his goal.

I will put an athlete under hypnosis and have him visualize scoring or winning, and the results are truly impressive. The necessary requirement is to *free* the players from being tensed up, get the player to feel harmony and to relax and be confident. That will enable the player to *do* it!

What the athlete must understand is that hypnosis is not magic nor supernatural power. It is simply a workable technique to get him to bring out his best. This, however, is quite enough. For, if one's game is beneath one's potential, we may well be talking about the difference between victory and defeat. As I have said, if one is not a great prizefighter he will not be able to be hypnotized to knock out a Joe Louis, Rocky Marciano or Muhammad Ali. He may, however, be brought to his best level, and find the confidence and energy to win fights he might otherwise have lost.

Going Under To Overcome

Today, in all types of sports, athletes are discovering the value of "mind games" in order to bring their performance to the peak level. Now it is widely recognized that athletic performance is not simply a matter of physical conditioning, but as well of mental input. It is especially important for the athlete to understand the contribution hypnosis can make.

Hypnosis when properly used—and it is by responsible certified hypnotherapists—can achieve positive results where more traditional approaches to problems have failed. Japanese business and industry set up hypnosis clinics to provide training for salespersons, to revitalize executive officers, and to maximize office worker efficiency. The Tokyo public schools used hypnosis to get students to relax, to increase academic performance, and to develop memory. A school in St. Louis employed hypnosis to increase learning motivation and ability to understand. Hypnosis can be used medically to cure diseases, and it can be used to deal with the fears and pain associated with dental work. It has been successful in helping children with problems of bedwetting, thumb sucking, hyperactivity, or poor grades. Gerontological problems such as insomnia, pain or senility have been dealt with by hypnosis. Hypnosis has been particularly successful with such disturbing problems as smoking, being overweight, nail biting, the pain of childbirth, and various sexual problems. Through hypnosis, removal of bad habits can be achieved, and good habits can be developed. This makes it a powerful weapon for the athlete.

For the athlete to appreciate hypnosis, it is important to understand what it is. A widespread misconception about hypnosis is that it is a technique of rendering subjects *unconscious*. This is not so. Even in the deepest levels of hypnosis the individual retains awareness. The very word "hypnosis" misleads us. It seems that the term "hypnosis" was coined by an English physician, Dr. James Braid, in 1843. The derivation of the name is from the Greek word "Hypnos," which was the name of the Greek God of Sleep.

People assume that being put into a hypnotic state is the same as being put to sleep. This is absolutely wrong. In fact, if one were sleeping one wouldn't be getting hypnotized.

Hypnosis is an altered state of consciousness, a trance state, but even in the deepest trance the subject can still hear the hypnotist. Far from putting one to sleep, it may be said that hypnosis is an awakening. For in inducing the altered state of consciousness of hypnotism, the hypnotist communicates *positive* messages directly to the unconscious, where they can be acted upon without hindrance by one's neurotic defenses. This is why the hypnotist can so effectively break through an athlete's hang-ups to plant helpful suggestions. Hypnosis is direct communication with the subconscious mind and, thus, motivates the individual on a deep level.

Now we have already seen how *meditation*, which is also an *altered state of consciousness*, can help individuals to refresh and get themselves together so they may be in top condition to achieve peak performance. The process of meditation takes one far away from one's problems, and thus produces a state of generalized relaxation. Hypnosis focuses in on one's problems, and thus enable's one to come directly to terms with them. Thus, hypnosis frees us from problems, so we can get out there and do it.

A highly effective and standard method of hypnotism used to create an altered state is known as *progressive relaxation*. A hypnotist will put a subject into a hypnotic state, deepening relaxation. The hypnotist will use imagery by creating a relaxing scene, perhaps in a pastoral setting or on the beach by the sea. Tranquil background music will do much to reinforce the atmosphere. A subliminal message can be communicated. In this context deep relaxation and an altered state of consciousness can be achieved.

The hypnotist, speaking in a quiet and calmly monotonous tone, will assure the subject that he will be more completely relaxed than ever before, and then will have him close his eyes, take two or three deep breaths, and begin an inner journey that will be totally refreshing. Here imagery will play a central role. The hypnotist will suggest the subject imagine in the form of seeing, hearing, and smelling in his mind some peaceful and beautiful setting. Transporting the subject to this blessed haven, he may then take him through a complete relaxation of every muscle and cell in his body, proceeding from head to toes. In doing this it may be helpful to countdown from 15 to 1, deepening the sense of relaxation on the countdown. At this point the subject will be very open and receptive to the positive suggestion that will alter his life for the better. In the case of an athlete, the hypnotist may implant suggestion to develop confidence and perfect his game. Post hypnotic suggestions can be provided to ensure there will be constant improvement. Upon achieving this, the hypnotist will slowly bring the subject out of the trance state.

As I have emphasized with other ways of developing mental and spiritual qualities, it is always best to find a qualified guide or instructor. There is an adage in law that a lawyer who defends his own case has a fool for a client. I do not feel one should go that far with mental and spiritual conditioning, but one should be very cautious in seeking to self-train. Thus, it is unquestionably good advice for any athlete or coach of a team to seek and explore the services of a competent hypnotist.

Having made clear my *reservations* about doing it on your own, I may now say, however, that it is not impossible to get involved in self training, and if you are really dedicated and determined, good results are certainly possible.

Self-hypnosis can be effectively practiced. It can best be taught by a professional hypnotist, and most serious athletes will follow that avenue. On the other hand, there are available many books and tapes, both audio and video, which can be effectively used as guides. We will now outline a reliable procedure to be followed for self-hypnosis.

What one has to practice is fixing attention, relaxing, and letting go. First, it is helpful for one to find a quiet place or room where you will be undisturbed and removed from noise; soothing background music may help, or a tape of natural sounds such as rainfall or an ocean can be used. Find a comfortable chair and sit in it, relaxed, with feet flat on the floor and hands in your lap. Close your eyes, and take three deep breaths. Then concentrate on all of your muscles in each part of your body, and relax each one. Concentrate, relaxing and letting each muscle become limp. Then, when you feel completely relaxed and are in a hypnotic state, you can *suggest* to yourself a specific word and implant the idea that whenever you say that word in the future you will feel instantly relaxed. You can insist you will accomplish all of your goals and be completely confident.

There are some standard means by which you can check to

determine if you are in a hypnotic state. Try to have your eyelids close by the time you count to ten. If you experience a strong urge to close your eyes before you reach the count of ten, or by the time you get to ten, then you know you are hypnotizing yourself. This is known as the *eye closure* test. A second test is the swallowing test. This time, as you count to ten, suggest you will feel terribly dry and get an irresistible urge to swallow, and afterwards you will return to normal. As you count and keep telling yourself, the need to swallow will become greater, and you will be putting yourself into a hypnotic state. In doing this test you must wait until you start swallowing even when not consciously telling yourself to do so. Then you know the swallowing is being controlled by your subconscious mind. At this point you can give yourself the necessary suggestions for your sports competition.

After putting yourself in the state of self-relaxation, you can specifically work on any problem you wish to solve. You may do this by using the eye closure method, and then suggest to yourself that you are now fully competent and prepared to solve your problem. You may examine every element of your problem, tracing it back into the past as far as necessary. This is called *hypnotic self-analysis*. This way you may discover why you are not hitting a baseball or golf ball in the way you need to.

There is no doubt that the athlete who realizes there is more to sports than being a beautiful body, who develops a philosophy, a way of living with a purpose—meditating, using visualization, and trying hypnosis—will lead himself to athletic excellence. Through it all, it is necessary to keep faith; that is, think positively.

You Are What You Think

The Power of Positive Thinking and Sports

There is an old Hungarian joke that serves as an excellent illustration of just how we can use our thinking against ourselves. If somebody says to you that you look like a horse, you think he's crazy, but if a second person mentions you look like a horse, you begin to wonder. If a third person tells you, "Hey, you look like a horse," you begin to worry. When a fourth person comes along and claims you look like a horse, you put on a saddle and start to neigh.

We very much are what we think, and if people can get us to think bad things about ourselves, we will be adversely affected by those things. If you leave your house feeling well and someone asks if you aren't feeling well, that will affect you. If in the course of the day, a few more persons remark about your not looking well, you may actually begin to feel ill. If your boss is unfair to you, your friends fail to support you, your mate is inconsiderate, and you experience frustrations and disappointments, you may begin to feel rumblings in your stomach or suffer headaches. If you begin to engage in a process of negative thinking, you actually program yourself to fail. If you get angry at someone and think all manner of terrible things about him, whom do you hurt? Not the object of your anger—he probably doesn't even know what is going on in your mind. So the irony is that you are mad at someone, wish to punish him, but hurt only yourself.

Negative thinking is destructive. It can make you sick. Just observe. Before you or someone else comes down with a cold, or some form of illness, there is usually a period when you feel down or are depressed. Negative thinking can lower our immune system and down we go. If you are in sports, you lose. Fortunately, there is a good medicine to remedy this. It is the power of *positive thinking*.

There is no question about it. If you have a positive attitude about achieving a goal, that will really help you do it. Negative self-conditioning has to be eliminated through positive thinking.

Thus one might simply say, "So, go ahead, start thinking positively." It is not, however, so simple. Somehow, in our world, most of us have so grown up thinking in such negative or self-defeating terms that we just have not the ability to break the habit and start thinking positively. In fact, for many to be told to think positively is like asking them to start speaking a foreign language with which they are unfamiliar. If someone wished to learn Hinduism, it wouldn't be very helpful to tell the person to do so by reading it in Sanskrit. If you haven't studied Sanskrit you will not be able to simply start reading it, and if you have spent most of your life thinking negatively, you just won't be able to start thinking positively. Often when someone is suffering from emotional problems, we say things such as, "Don't be nervous," or "Pull yourself together." The guy is falling apart and someone is telling him to pull himself together. It is ridiculous. The person must be taught how to deal with his nerves. And for those who are not achieving peak performance in life or sports, it is necessary to be taught how to think positively.

The great Stoic philosopher Seneca told us it is part of the cure to wish to be cured. And, ironically, not everyone does wish to be cured. There are many who wish to fall ill, for that makes it possible to feel sorry for oneself, to escape responsibilities. Thus, one has to develop the will to wish to be cured, to wish to win.

To start with, we must come to understand that we never say "Oh, I cannot do that. I know how I am, and I just am not good at something like that." We must understand, "Nothing is, but thinking makes it so." If we think bad things, we will make it so. If we think good things, we also can make it so.

We must learn to develop habits of positive thinking. James Allen was one of the great expounders of *"The Power of Positive Thinking,"* the philosophy of such men as Norman Vincent Peale. Allen says that one only begins to be when he or she stops complaining. One of the prime requirements in developing oneself is to stop accusing others of being responsible for faults or problems or losing. Instead of looking for the source of your problems in others, search within for your own hidden powers and talents. According to James Allen, impure thoughts lead to enervating and confusing habits, while thoughts of fear, doubt and indecision lead to weakness and failure. Thus, one has to start thinking about beautiful things, and have gentle, loving and unselfish thoughts. Allen claims there is no physician like cheerful thought. What one must make an effort to do is to think well of all, and to be cheerful with all. For this one must banish thoughts of doubt and fear. One must specifically direct his or her thoughts toward desired goals. There has to be a purpose, or a goal, otherwise one will flounder in aimlessness and indecision.

These ideas, expressed in James Allen's book *As A Man Thinketh*, are directly relevant to all athletic experience. If the athlete lets any doubts seep into his mind, they will be enough to result in defeat. In his *Yoga Sutras*, the great yogic teacher Patanjali teaches that foremost in one's spiritual development one must attain a state of mental purity. He directs us to replace destructive and negative thoughts with constructive and positive reflections. If you have a thought of anger or hatred, replace it with one of love. A thought of fear must be replaced with one of courage, selfishness with unselfishness.

One way to make it easier to banish impure thoughts by pondering *contrary* thoughts is by accepting one's lot in life instead of feeling sorrow for oneself because there were not good breaks. Be content with what you have and then work upon that to improve it. To allow oneself self-pitying feelings just drains one. Therefore, one should count one's blessings and add to them. Instead of complaining about what one doesn't have, one should get to work at achieving desirable goals.

One excellent method for strengthening oneself in order to reach peak performance consists in dwelling upon *any* good things that are in your life and feeling gratitude for them. The

Chinese say it is easier to light a single candle than to curse the darkness. Cursing the darkness drains us and puts us down. Thinking of any beneficial thing lifts us up and brings light into our life. Think of someone you love. Bring that person into your heart. Then bring others you love into your heart. Soon you will find your heart expanding, and will have the strength to invite into your heart people you do not even like. When you do that, enemies will no longer disturb you and you will be stronger. You will be a better person instead of a bitter person. You will become a more perfect athlete. Soon you will stop sending yourself messages that make you feel inadequate and thus, incompetent.

Filling up with positive feelings and love feelings, you can send yourself good messages and become a winner. Imagine yourself performing the way you want to and soon you will *do it*.

Remember, in a previous chapter I said it is important to have a philosophy, by which I meant some sense of purpose. This makes it possible for one to set a definite goal. Without a definite goal one becomes directionless, and thus cannot concentrate his or her energy. It is in the light of a specific goal to achieve that one can come to develop a *mission*. One has a mission to achieve something. That will motivate him or her to do good, and in terms of that he or she will think positively. In the 1984 Olympics, Mary Lou Retton the gymnast, revealed that she actually *mind-scripted* every move the very night before she won a gold medal.

The yield of high energy will result from reorienting yourself to a positive frame of mind. And, as you have seen, a positive frame of mind can be built from positive thinking. This may also be reinforced by a technique sports psychologist Bruce Ogilvie uses, called *self-talk*, as well as by positive *body language*.

Self-talk involves rewriting the script one usually uses in talking to opposing athletes or in dealing with obstacles in sports. One can unconsciously become very negative in the words he or she uses to address competitors in sports, or to describe problems encountered. A ballplayer might even get angry at his bat or the baseball. He may use hostile words in conjunction with them. What he might do then is apply the method of *contraries* I spoke of, and develop self-talk to it. He might speak to the bat or ball affectionately as a dear friend.

An athlete may engage in dangerous, negative self-talk about his abilities. He may say to himself such things as, "I am getting too old," or "I am passing my prime," or "this match is too difficult," or "I really wasn't ready," or "I am not fast enough," or "I cannot get in good enough shape for this one." Athletes do engage in negative self-talk, and it does damage their performance. An athlete cannot carry the weight of those negative thoughts into a competition.

Negative thought patterns, therefore, must be replaced with affirmations. The first thing is to catch yourself red-handed in the self-crime of assaulting your confidence. Become conscious of every negative idea you plant within yourself and, with patience rather than anger, restructure your ideas to be affirmative. Tell yourself confidently, "I can do it!" Repeat to yourself all of your virtues, and they will become strengthened. Talk about the athletic tools you use in an affectionate way as you would talk about a close friend or lover. Use these endearing terms, and you will begin to shift negative feelings into positive ones.

Reinforce this shift with vitamin "L". And what is vitamin "L"? It is *laughter*! An excellent way to set positive thinking into motion is a *simple smile*. Just smiling actually sends nerve signals from muscles in the face to the limbic system, the core of emotions in our brain. Therefore, when one simply smiles positive results occur. The opposite results are set in motion by frowning, and a tensed-up condition results. And when one actually laughs, it has been shown that more oxygen gets into his or her lungs, breathing becomes deeper, and circulation improves. A new book by British author Liz Hodgkinson is called *Smile Therapy*, and it details the benefits of smiling and laughing. Laughter expands blood vessels, and this brings more blood to the hands and feet.

A psychiatrist at Stanford Medical School named William Fry has established that laughing a couple hundred times a day is as good for a person as ten minutes of rowing. When one laughs, heart rate increases, blood pressure rises, breathing quickens and he or she takes in more oxygen. Laughing affects all parts of the body, and works it out. Then when the laughter stops, one will go into a nice relaxation. It all serves to put one in a positive frame of mind.

When one smiles or laughs, he feels more confident. Thus, positive thinking is developed through such devices as dwelling on positive ideas, using self-talk, smiling and laughing. Posture also plays a role. Standing erect, chest out, shoulders back exudes confidence. Slumped shoulders or slouching leads to negative attitudes.

In developing positive thinking, one also can employ what psychologists refer to as *aversive conditioning*. When one starts getting negative ideas, one must do something to create a negative association. Thus, if a self-defeating idea enters the mind, one might stick oneself with a pin or pinch oneself. Soon this pattern of thinking will lose appeal.

Another tributary flowing into the river of positive thinking is that of lucid dreaming. Athletes never believed the mile could be run in four minutes, as we have seen, but what really got them was when they found out you can be awake while dreaming and sound a sleep. Dr. Stephen La Berge of the Stanford University Sleep Research Center informs us:

> "I could think as clearly as ever, freely remember details of my waking life, and act deliberately upon conscious reflection. Yet none of this diminished the vividness of my dream. Paradox or no, I was awake in my dream! [1]

Many exciting things can happen in the dream state. Robert Louis Stevenson got his famous *The Strange Case of Dr. Jekyll and Mr. Hyde* from a dream. Scientist Friedrick August Kekule discovered the structure of the benzene molecule in a dream. Great musical composers such as Beethoven and Mozart received inspiration from their dreams. How is this applied to sports? Golfer Jack Nicklaus found out something in a dream that improved his game *overnight* by ten strokes.

The trick is to learn to recognize that we are dreaming while our dream is still in progress. This is "lucid dreaming." In lucid dreaming you are *asleep* with respect to the physical world, but *awake* in regard to the inner world of your dreams. In other words, while sleeping and dreaming you remain conscious to the fact you are sleeping and dreaming. Being aware you are dreaming gives you the power to face fears directly and seek to overcome them, and take them over into the waking state.

To learn how to have a *lucid dream* it is essential to learn how to *recall* your dreams. In order to remember your dreams, an *essential requirement* is to have the *specific intention* to do so. *Keep* reminding yourself of this intention before going to bed. Provide strength for your resolve to remember by keeping a dream journal by your bed. Every time you awaken record whatever you can remember of your dreams. The more dreams you record, the more you will be able to remember. You must read over the journal. The more you become familiar with what your dreams are like, the more you will develop the ability to recognize one while it is still happening, and thereby to be awake while dreaming.

Let it be your first thought upon awakening to ask, "What was I dreaming?" Eventually you will be able to master the ability of being awake while dreaming. Now once you've really developed a strong *intention* to have a lucid dream, you must verbalize the following:

> "Next time I am dreaming, I want to remember to recognize I am dreaming."[2]

Building up the capacity to think and fell *positively* while *awake* and *asleep* will enable one to engage in athletic activity with his or her full being, and to master difficult situations. To summarize, one may say that perfection of positive thinking involves thinking good and happy thoughts, using *self-talk*, using smile and laugh *therapy*, combining it with *aversive* conditioning, and using *lucid dreaming*. In addition to these, get into the habit of always using *positive words*. Do not make excuses and never employ negative terms. Along with positive *thinking*, there must go *positive speaking*. And, one must set a *goal* in order to be positive about where he is going. Finally to return to the theme of a previous chapter, one can bring what is *positive* to the sharpest focus through *visualization*.

Visualization is virtually essential to the athlete and has already worked wonders with many great athletes. Karen Krofanta and Hank Taubler, who coached the Olympic slalom racing team for the United States, got each participant to *visualize* the course to be skied. Psychologist Richard Suinn had each athlete he worked with develop the precise imagery that worked best for him or her.

Michael Murphy taught visualization for achievement in golf and Mike Spino used relaxation and visualization to develop running.[3] Bernie Zilbergeld and Arnold A. Lazarus informs us:

> "Greg Louganis, another gold medalist and the only diver ever to score a perfect 10 in international competition, employed as much mental training as physical training. He visualized each dive as he wanted it to be, step by step, 40 times before mounting the platform. Similar stories about the value of mental training were told by skiers, weight lifters, hurdlers, boxers, and just about everyone else. [4]

Further we learn that Colorado State University psychologist

Richard M. Suinn, in research on U.S. Olympians in Nordic skiing, the biathlon, and the pentathlon, "has found that visualizing an event in the controlled dream state marshals the involvement of the body on the deepest levels."

Not long ago, an Alpine ski racer visualized a race course, and as he went through the imagery, Suinn measured the racer's muscle activity with electrodes. Then Suinn asked the athlete to describe the course verbally. "I found," says Suinn, "that I could match his verbal description with the bursts of muscle activity recorded during the visualization. For example, he described an area where he jumped into the air, and we got a burst of activity at that point. When he described a bumpy part of the course, there was activity again."[5]

The verdict is in: Think positively, and *you can do it*!

Your Body's Mind

THE BODY HAS A MIND OF ITS OWN

Thus far I have concentrated upon the importance of mental training for the development of athletic prowess. The value of such training cannot be overemphasized. As you have been observing, it is now well established that mental concentration and positive thinking can produce amazing results for our bodies. The consummate athlete needs not just brawn but brain—wisdom! While realizing this, however, you should not lose sight of the fact that the body is amazing in its own right. The body has a wisdom of its own. For the athlete to attain full command of all his or her potential, this wisdom of the body should be understood.

Probably no one was more responsible than W.B. Cannon for making us aware that the body has a mind of its own. His book was appropriately called *The Wisdom of the Body*! Balance is an essential ingredient of wisdom. The wise person gets in balance with life and the cosmos. The body keeps its processes in balance all of the time. Cannon called the coordination of physiological processes "homeostasis." It is all rather marvelous. If one bleeds, the body responds by producing coagulation. If the heat that is a natural consequence of a maximum use of the muscles over a 20 minute period wasn't quickly dissipated, some of the albuminous substances of the body would coagulate as if it were a hard-boiled egg. Homeostasis, the wisdom of the body, is ever restoring the body to a normal state in reaction to any disturbance of its function.

If a disease agent enters your body there are certain white blood cells that surround and digest them. There is a different kind of white blood cell that forms *antibodies*. Antibodies are protein substances that identify and destroy specific bacteria. And then there are white blood cells that help in clotting and healing wounds. All white blood cells exist in bone marrow and lymph tissue, and are produced to do combat with infection.

The body often knows what to do in a better and more efficient way than a trained doctor. If the body has this mind of its own and wisdom, it is certainly important for the successful athlete to know as much about it as he can in order to perform in harmony with it. The natural athlete has to learn to follow the natural working of the body in order to give the best performance of which he is capable.

A great German historian named Oswald Spengler wrote a book called *The Decline of the West*. He saw the *clock* as a central symbol in Western civilization. We all organize, schedule our lives in terms of it. It is based not upon a natural flow, however, but on a mechanical division of units of measurement. Since most of us live by time, by clocks, we do not even realize that our own bodies have a natural rhythm, a time all of their own. In a highly significant study called *Body Time*,

THE BODY HAS A MIND OF ITS OWN

Gay Gaer Luce shows that physiological rhythms are as much a part of our structure as bones and flesh. This being the case it is clear that to maintain our health and well-being, and certainly to be good athletes, we must become aware of our natural physiological rhythms and try to get into sync with them.

Time structure gives our life shape. Gay Gaer Luce observes, "invisible rhythms underlie most of what we assume to be constant in ourselves and the world around us."[2] Any event recurring at a given interval may be regarded as a cycle. Many of our functions are in rhythmical patterns, cycles.

Many human physiological functions display a *circadian* rhythm, that is, a *daily* one. Performance ability is correlated with our bodily cycles, and thus there will be a given time, afternoon or evening, when an athlete will attain optimum level of achievement. Thus, it will be most important for an athlete to discover how his or her particular muscular coordination and strength vary in each 24-hour period.

A most important development based on the understanding that one operates in terms of biological clocks, biological cycles, was the *biorhythm theory*. Biorhythms are based on one's physical, emotional and intellectual cycles, which determine how one feels. By charting these biorhythms and seeing how they develop, one can get in charge of his or her life.

The biorhythm theory assumes there are three powerful cycles or rhythms in everyone. These biorhythms begin the moment one is born. One's clock is set at that instant and runs regularly for the remainder of his or her life. There are three primary biorhythmic cycles: the *physical*, the *emotional* and the *intellectual*. They all start at the same time, but are of different length.

The *first* cycle is the *physical cycle*. It lasts for 23 days. It is the basis for physical strength and endurance. The first 11 1/2 days are referred to as *discharge* days. This is so because during this period the muscles release or discharge their stored energy. When this cycle peaks, it goes into decline for the next 11 1/2 days. This is called the *recharging period*. During this phase of the cycle muscle cells rest and regain strength.

The *second* cycle is the *emotional*, the sensitivity or female cycle. It is 28 days. The first 14 days of this cycle are the *discharge* days. These mark the positive phase. In this period emotional energy reaches a high point. The individual becomes more "cheerful" and optimistic.

The *third* cycle is the mental cycle. It is a long one, lasting 33 days. The first half of it is the period of *discharge*. It is in this phase that intellectual energy is in a thriving state. The second half of the 33 days is the *recharge* period. Learning, whether academic or athletic should be concentrated in the *plus* or *discharge* period. Many biorhythm experts advise that basic decisions should not be made on days when emotional or mental energy is on the minus side of the cycle. Biorhythm researchers have discovered that people tend to have more accidents on the physical and emotional downside of a biorhythm cycle.

Biorhythms have a very natural application to sports. It is particularly important for training. Athletes do have ups and downs, and during a down period training may become terribly burdensome. Other times training will be a "piece of cake" for an athlete.

A biorhythm chart for an athlete is a means for predicting when good and bad days will come, and thus make it possible to adjust accordingly.

The Body Has A Mind Of Its Own

In their book *Biorhythms*, Barbara O'Neil and Richard Phillips have discussed the application of biorhythms to sports. Johnny Miller in the 1973 U.S. Open Gold Tournament became the U.S. Open champion. According to his biorhythm chart at that point his level of competitive performance was high. Stil,l that was not his high-point on the chart, and in fact he only won by one point. On his peak day he might have done even better. Thus following a biorhythm chart gives the athlete the chance to work with the best odds.

Billie Jean King defeated Bobby Riggs in tennis when her energies were high, and it has been said Bobby Riggs was biorhythmically low.

Of course, a *biorhythm* chart guarantees nothing, and doesn't mean anyone has to be good or bad on any given day. What it does mean, however, is that certain days will be more favorable or plus days, while other days will be more unfavorable, and that we should keep an eye on these times so that we can better deal with any given situation.

Biorhythm charts can be easily enough worked out by oneself. There are a number of books that explain how in simple terms, such as *Biorhythms* by O'Neil and Phillips, *Biorhythms in Your Life* by Daniel Cohen, or *Is This Your Day* by George S. Thommen.

The wisest course, however, would be to have a chart done professionally. There are many sources that provide that service, and they are not difficult to find. Thus in connection with a training program, an athlete might be well advised to check that out.

The master athlete might not only use biorhythms but also *biofeedback*. If the body has a rhythm and wisdom of its own, it is of great importance for one to read its messages. Marvin Karlins and Lewis M. Andrews say that *biofeedback* "is simply a particular *kind* of feedback—feedback from different parts of our body - the brain, the heart, the circulatory system, the different muscle groups and so on. Biofeedback training is the procedure that allows us to tune into our bodily functions and, eventually, to control them."[4] They continue to say that biofeedback is necessary if one is ever to gain mastery over every aspect of his behavior.

Unconscious body states give off energy that is capable of being measured. Thus a minute rise in hand temperature produces more heat from the hand. An increase in muscle tension causes more electrical activity at the surface of the skin. Now a biofeedback machine monitors these slight energy shifts, and turns them out as light flashes or clicking sounds people can perceive with their five senses.

The point of biofeedback is to get an individual to recognize his own body waves in order that he may control them. What happens is that his body is feeding back information to him so that he can be master of his body. Some particular function of the body is monitored by an instrument which can sense, by electrodes, signals concerning such bodily functions as heart rate, blood pressure, muscle tension or the brain wave state.

It was always taught in Western science that there could be no conscious control of internal physiological functions. By keeping track of what his or her body is doing it is possible for individuals to do something about it, to change it in a desired manner.

A Dr. Whatmore in Seattle, who does biofeedback training with patients, has coined a term to describe a problem people have of doing bad things to themselves. His term is "dysponesis." *Dys* means wrong or faulty and *ponos* means energy. People do self-defeating or even self-destructive things by misusing their energy. Perhaps an athlete who is under stress or nervous because of a coming event will brace him or herself by raising his blood pressure or pouring more adrenalin into his system; or, the athlete might exaggerate his fears of the competition. In such a case biofeedback achieves what nothing else can. It identifies and controls negative or self-defeating bracing efforts.

What biofeedback researchers have learned is that by concentrating on a given function a person can change. Thus if the message comes through that one's body is doing something it should not, through biofeedback that can be changed by concentrated effort. Jodi Lawrence comments, "Cues, like a sound or tone, signal what's happening as your mind or body actions are translated into sensory signals helping you to control the internal action."[5]

It is pointed out that Dr. Elmer Green taught people how to control their finger temperatures while simultaneously reducing the skin temperature of their foreheads. By learning this it might be possible to cure migraine headaches. This method can result in a decrease of vascular congestion, a regularizing of the vascular supply to the brain and head, thereby eliminating migraine.

One of the greatest benefits of biofeedback is that it can alter consciousness and thereby elevate one to a higher mental state, a deeply serene and relaxed condition. Insofar as a relaxed state is very important for an athlete, biofeedback can be of much value in putting oneself in a proper emotional frame for athletic events.

There are four kinds of brain waves. They are beta, alpha, theta and delta. *Delta* brain waves are the slowest, and are prominent in deep *sleep*. *Theta* brain waves are present in a drowsy state or a dream state. *Beta* waves are the fastest, and are produced in a waking state and during stressful periods. *Alpha* waves occur when one is fully awake and yet as relaxed as when sleeping peacefully.

Alpha state is highly desirable for athletic performance. Being too tight or stressful can hinder successful competition. The special value of biofeedback is that it can quickly and easily get one in a meditative state. I myself have often used biofeedback to promote peak performance in sports, and I am eminently pleased with the results.

Now biofeedback devices are available at low cost, and it is not difficult for one to master the technique, but it's much better for the successful athlete to work with a psychologist who has professional biofeedback skills or with a biofeedback technician. The result will be a tranquil state, without drugs, and better control of one's body.

The importance of a tranquil or relaxed condition cannot be overemphasized for the master athlete. While it was once believed physical power and strength were primary, it is now recognized that a relaxed and loose condition in which one can flow with the rhythm of life best prepares one for athletic activity. In his book *The Warrior Athlete* Dan Millman makes this eminently clear:

> Men develop great bulk and perform feats of brute strength, as in weight lifting, but in lightness, speed, and most economic use of

strength, it may be the women athletes who will shine, because they tend to develop less muscular tension.⁶

Millman calls our attention to the cat. You never see any muscle-bound cats, and you never see any athlete who could equal the accomplishments of a cat in its movements. A cat can just be sitting there on the ground and suddenly spring ten feet up. The cat keeps relaxed, and doesn't carry tension.

It has even been realized by the Chinese in their development of the martial arts that the ideal of the perfect martial artist is to imitate the swift and beautiful movements of the animals. Particularly in the Japanese aikido it is understood that sheer physical power is self-defeating. The aikido master uses the strength of his opponent. It is the aikido master's animal like movements not his power that enables him to be triumphant.

In the old physics, based on the work of Newton, everything was understood in terms of matter, force and mechanics. In the world of physics after Einstein and quantum mechanics, fluid energy and vibrations become fundamental. In his *The Ultimate Athlete*, George Leonard makes the point, "The human individual is viewed here as an *energy being*, a center of vibrancy, emanating waves that radiate out through space and time, waves that respond to and interact with myriad other waves. The physical body is seen as one manifestation of the total energy being, co-existing with the Energy Body."⁷

Much evidence has been accumulated to indicate that surrounding our physical body there is an aura of energy. Two Russians, the Kirlians, actually developed a technique called Kirlian photography with which they could photograph this energy. Thus, even in talking about the body we are not dealing with something hard, solid and static, but with energy, a process. This is what makes aikido such an incredible form of self defense. The Japanese learn to work with a basic energy of our being, which they call *ki*. To relax and let the *ki*, flow; that energy giving strength is what enables an aikido master to fend off attack from several persons at one time.

The point is that to do well in sports involves getting your energy in harmony and balance. In aikido you have to think of a cosmic energy, *Ki*, filling your body; keep supple and relax, and let the ki pour forth, and an attacker cannot harm you.

A great shift is occurring on the athletic landscape, a shift away from blockbuster physical power to movement and dynamic energy. Dyveke Spino teaches tennis in terms of what she calls *Tennis Flow*. The emphasis is on flowing with energy rather than using aggressive movements. In aikido it is emphasized that one has to conquer not so much an outside opponent but oneself. It is the same in all sports. Dyveke Spino sees a problem prevalent in tennis in that players fight against the ball, try too hard, employ too much force, and thus muscles become tense and rigid. Tennis players allow themselves to get angry and tight. Ms. Dyveke Spino teaches players to meditate and loosen up. To do well in sports it is necessary to free energy and loosen up.

The strange thing is that these teachings, which may seem esoteric, do work. If you are trying to resist someone bending your arm and try to stand solid in terms of physical strength, the resistance will falter. If, however, you relax and consciously see or feel *ki*, energy giving you strength, your arm will be much more difficult to bend.

THE BODY HAS A MIND OF ITS OWN

There are exercises people can learn and training that can be undertaken, but *above all* what must be emphasized is the *necessity* for a change of *attitude*. You try to use your strength and try to defeat someone, and then you tense up and your muscles tense up. You lose your own center of gravity. If you take it easy, stay lose, but feel confident and strong, and really believe you are calling up your *ki* energy and extending it outward, you will find a new capacity to achieve your goals.

There are doubtless too many ideas in your head that stand between you and your body. They may block the wisdom of the body. The mind doesn't "hear" the wisdom of the body, and then you get out of shape, get a tennis elbow, a bad back, or put on excess weight. You have got to still the mind and concentrate on messages from the body. It's a matter of changing attitudes to go more with life instead of trying too hard, and ending up going against life.

There is a program called *Rolfing,* and what it involves is getting your *body integrated* and *aligned,* and getting your *mind integrated* and *aligned*. According to Ida Rolf, much of this has to do with getting yourself lined up properly with gravity. If the way you sit, stand, walk, run, carry yourself is out of line with gravity, then your mind will be misaligned and trouble will ensue. Ida Rolf's prescription consisted of a method she called *structural integration*. Structural integration is a means of manipulating the body to put it in alignment with gravity.

People waste energy and create muscular tension in doing the most ordinary and simple things—getting up from a chair or sitting down in it, using a knife and fork, lifting a bag of groceries. In doing these things, improper movements are made and muscles are tensed that should not be used. If there is poor posture, then the body is out of line with gravity, and excess energy is needed to keep stable.

Whereas the psychologist or psychiatrist may assume one's body is just an outward manifestation of the personality, of the mind or emotions, Ida Rolf regards the *physical body* as the personality. Rolf's approach is to get the body balanced and integrated, and through doing that, to get the whole person in condition.

People do not unify their body parts and the mechanisms of the body. It is betrayed in the smallest acts. Eyes appear drowsy or strained, standing up or walking shows awkwardness, speech is not a product of a unified person. It is almost as if a person has gone to sleep. *Rolfing* is a way of *reawakening*.

Tension builds up in muscles, and they become contracted in an unhealthy orientation. Rolfing releases chronically contracted muscles, and in doing so enables the body to return to its natural harmony. What is happening is that the person is getting unblocked physically. Breathing becomes natural again. Metabolism, the muscles, the cells, all of the body finds its energy recharged.

Inelastic muscle tissue is released and charged with new energy. Muscles expand, and the whole body becomes realigned and balanced. What happens to one in life places great burdens upon the body. An insult, a frustration, anger results in our tensing our body, and in time that tenseness, stiffness, or inelasticity hardens into our body structure. We carry indignities around in our bodies like heavy weights. Shoulders droop, the body leans forward, one tends to become bent over, the chest sinks in, muscles thicken, and as a corollary, our emotions also become inelastic and worn down. We do let ourselves get into bad shape. How can Rolfing reshape us?

Much is based upon the muscles. Muscles are groups of fibers held together by *fasciae*. The *myofasciae* are tissues that surround and give support to bundles of muscles. The myofasciae are plastic, and therefore can be shaped. Rolfing works on this myofascial system. Rolfing usually commences with 10 hour long sessions. During these sessions Rolf processing involves getting muscles that have hardened into inelasticity to let go of tension and become free. As they become free they lengthen, and the skeletal frame and organs adapt to a more harmonious and natural relation.

A person doing Rolfing will manipulate the fasciae and massage so as to reposition muscles and ligaments. Balance is restored and one feels it is possible to breathe freely again. The whole body, emotions and mind become integrated in a healthy way. When you are out of balance, you tend to stay out of balance, but when you get into balance and aligned to gravity, you tend to remain in it.

Getting aligned with gravity is important for all of us, but essential to the athlete, and thus Rolfing is something, along with other programs we have covered, he or she may wish to explore.

Another interesting approach with the aim of aligning us with gravity is that of Dr. Feldenkrais. His method is one of making us more sensitive, and is more gentle and easier than Ida Rolf's. If you are lying down or sitting down, the trick is not to spring up or jump up suddenly. The point is not to strain. Movements should flow and be natural. The body must be patterned so it will follow the most economical path of movement. Movements are thus small and easy and relaxed. They release us. These are subtle movements that make us more supple and sensitive, and thus develop a kind of artistry of our bodies which serves us well in sports. Sports trainers have used the Feldenkrais technique and helped restore bodies in football, hockey and wrestling.

In considering the importance of our bodies, of aligning them with gravity and getting them to work more naturally, we must always keep in mind the central significance of breathing. It's amazing that in a world stressing education, we learn so many complicated and difficult things, but we get to college and still do not know how to breathe properly.

A physiotherapist, Magda Proskauer, has devoted particular attention to breathing. She employs breathing to put a person back into contact with his or her body. She uses breathing therapy because she has found that every part of the body from head to toe is affected by the flow of breath.

The importance of breathing cannot be overestimated. Breathing in air is our means of supplying our bloodstream with the oxygen it requires in order to nourish it, and through it to further nourish tissues, glands, nerves and vital organs.

It is said that we are what we eat, and, perhaps, it should also be said that we are what we breathe. If the blood does not get the oxygen it requires from our breathing, our digestion will fail. It is also said that we are what we think, but without sufficient or good quality air, we cannot think properly. To work as it should, the brain needs three times as much oxygen as the rest of the body.

We breathe more than 2,000 times per day. People can go as

much as a month without food and can go three days without drink, but without breath we are thinking in terms of minutes. In breathing we take in *oxygen* and clean out of our system *carbon dioxide*. If we get no oxygen and are left with the poisonous waste gas of carbon dioxide, we will die; and what is more, if we fail to get enough oxygen we will only half live. *Humans* must exhale *carbon dioxide*, but *plants* must inhale *carbon dioxide*. The plants convert the carbon dioxide into carbohydrates, and these then release oxygen into the air. Plants, trees, animals are all interdependent. The bottom line of all this is that we must have oxygen and breathing to live well; the more properly we breathe the better we will live, and for the athlete proper breathing is absolutely essential to peak performance. And that brings us back to Magda Proskauer.

Magda Proskauer gets the individual to observe the breathing process as it moves in and out of the lungs. Just passively watching is an important first step. She has people at first lie on their backs, resting and close the eyes. This is a proper condition in which to be to become aware of the breath.

Magda Proskauer tries to get people to become sensitive to the natural rhythm of breath. She has people get their breath out in staccato fashion, emptying the lungs in short and speedy gushes. After the lungs are thus cleaned out, the point is not to *consciously breathe* in, but just allow the air to naturally flow in. Then the person comes to appreciate how breath can move on its own. When the lungs fill, in accord with the rhythm of life, they just naturally proceed to empty out. The point is to deprogram ourselves of our conditioned manner of breathing, and to get in harmony with the natural pattern of breathing.

When one learns how to breathe naturally, then one can learn to so expand and contract the lungs in such a way as to involve the whole body. As free flow of the breath becomes established, one becomes calmer and lives more fully. In athletic performance, no energy is wasted.

Many have now come forth to proclaim that we are living in a *New Age*. This New Age is a time in which many traditional values and relationships are undergoing *transformation*. In war we know that if we resort to brute power, our maximum potential for destruction, we can blow the world to bits. Thus the nation with the greatest physical power, realizing the self-destructive character of such power, often becomes powerless. Massive power may be too inflexible, and *new strategies* are adopted against great powers, such as guerrilla warfare or terrorism. It is a different way of using power or energy, but can be very effective. Gandhi also rendered great powers helpless by using moral strength as opposed to brute military strength.

It worked. Martin Luther King used a similar strategy in our own society. In aikido and judo the power of the opponent is turned against him. In Zen it is taught that the powerful oak tree is blown down in a hurricane, but the palm tree swaying with the wind remains. And in our New Age sports has benefited from all of this wisdom. As we have seen, the master athlete must think of the body not in terms of a powerful musculature, of large muscles, of a great rooted tree, but in terms of dynamic *energy*, in terms of suppleness and speed. In Japan the aikido master stands straight, but *relaxed* rather than *stiff*. In him there is a power of energy rather than static physical force.

The Body Has A Mind Of Its Own

One of the most excellent ways to perfect the body for competition is to learn the practice of an ancient Chinese way of exercise called t'ai chsi ch'uan. A Western woman, Sophia Delza, who has become master of this system has explained its advantages.

She points out that we in the West *overdo* in our exercises and sports. We make the error of thinking of strength in terms of hard and tense movements and the ability to expend energy violently. The philosophy of t'ai chi ch'uan, on the contrary, shows how energy can be controlled, strength balanced, and vitality stabilized by *using* the body so as *not* to strain muscles, *not* to *overactivate* the heart, and *not* to engage in excessive exertion.

T'ai chi ch'uan is a way of learning to meditate while in *motion* by focusing upon one's energy flow. Central to t'ai chi ch'uan is chi, which as an *internal energy*, is quite similar to the Japanese *ki*. To get in contact with this energy, t'ai chi ch'uan starts out with *relaxation*. Ch'uan itself means "fist," but does not denote as in the West aggressive attack. Rather it means concentration and containment. Ch'uan implies the control or containment of matter by spirit.

Ch'uan is a way of organizing harmonious forms. It is continuous action with each movement growing out of what it is joined to. Thus, no movement is isolated but all flow harmoniously together as in a stream.

The benefits are substantial. Sophia Delza lists some. As with physical exercise, blood circulation is increased, glands are aided, muscles are nourished, and the nervous system is stimulated, and all without increasing the activity of the heart or breathing rhythm.

The practitioner of t'ai chi ch'uan learns to open every part of the body so chi can flow harmoniously. Eventually one will develop the capacity to direct chi to any part of the body in need of replenishment. The spine is especially important and must be exercised so chi can travel along it up to the head. To achieve this, no matter what one is doing, one must ever concentrate on *chi*.

When one reaches the highest stages, one can become like a child. A child breathes naturally, not from high up on the chest but in the abdomen, and meets challenges *relaxed*. An infant's grasp of the finger is really strong, but not stiff or tense because relaxed energy is the basis.

Standard t'ai chi ch'uan practice teaches 128 postures. These have been cut down to 37 *essential* ones. There are many excellent books and articles which precisely describe basic motions. There are, however, instruction centers in most urban centers, and t'ai chi ch'uan would be best assimilated by getting involved in this practice. No matter which sport he or she engages in, the practice of t'ai chi ch'uan would definitely increase ability and bring enrichment to the athlete.

Now, one may contemplate with utmost contentment many of the mental and bodily techniques I have discussed in a relaxing flotation tank. Whether you find *biorhythms, biofeedback, Rolfing, rhythmic breathing* or *t'ai chi ch'uan* helpful to you, it is possible to attain a higher state of tranquility, while considering them, in a *flotation tank*.

A flotation tank looks like a very big plastic egg. About nine feet in length and four to six feet in width, they are filled with a foot of water and about 100 pounds of epsom salts. The temperature of the water is maintained at the level of skin temperature. Your body cannot sink in it, and thus you *float*.

Tanks usually have an underwater sound system so it is possible to listen to soothing music or programmed messages, providing confidence and inculcating an affirmative attitude for some sporting event. The tank may also provide a video screen, and while peacefully floating, an athlete can watch a video tape offering instructions on effective methods and techniques of various athletic games.

Also effective in a flotation tank are guided visualization cassettes. In the highly relaxed state attained in a flotation tank, visualization messages are quite effective, penetrating deep into the unconscious. You remain in the tank for about an hour, and when you leave you should feel positive, as if you have been recharged.

To get the mind and body together is essential to achievement of high level athletic performance. The athlete therefore must take good care of his mind and body, and follow methods which integrate one mentally, spiritually and physically. In this rigorous program of finding personal and athletic fulfillment, nutrition must play a central role.

BEYOND MCDONALDS AND DUNKIN DONUTS
Nutrition and Sports

To excel in sports it is important to eat properly, never overeat, and avoid junk food. We all know that. One day right before a big game, the great home run hitter Babe Ruth ate 20 hot dogs. The heavyweight boxer who fought and beat the best, Tony Galento, did more than Babe Ruth. Tony Galento put down into his stomach 52 hot dogs before going into a fight in which he put down his opponent.[1] Of course, hot dogs are fatty junk food. Despite the terrible eating habits of these two athletic giants, it is definitely not advised for anyone to eat 52 hot dogs before any competition. Anyhow, who knows what Galento would have achieved if he had not? Very exceptional individuals can *sometimes* break rules. It is, however, following the correct rules that will lead to success. Following the *crazy* things a champion may do will not lead to championship. It will lead to making you crazy. Muhammad Ali was a great fighter, and one of the things that contributed to the fact he was not in good shape by the time of his last fight, which he lost, was a wrong type of diet.[2]

Eating an improper diet may do harm even to a champion like Muhammad Ali. Also, carefully eating healthy food can really work. Wayne Stetina, a great distance bicycle rider, is a vegetarian and is scrupulously careful about his diet.

Tatsuro Hirooka took over as manager of the Seibu Lions, a professional Japanese baseball team in October 1981. The only distinction the Lions had at the time was that they had just finished *last* in the Pacific League. In fact, the Lions were so bad that they were regarded as a laughingstock. Tatsuro Hirooka, however, didn't think anything about the Lions was very funny. He decided to get the Lions out of the laughable cellar and back up to the respectable top.

What did Hirooka do? The *first* thing he did was not to roar at the Lions to play better baseball, but to get them to *eat better food*. He demanded his new team cut way down on meat, and cut out white rice and sugar. In the beginning he ordered the team to go on a diet of whole grains, tofu and fish. In a short time he restricted the Lions to a diet of nothing but vegetable and soy products.

The team seemed to think they must have been cursed. The had fallen into last place, and now their manager was some kind of nut. Hirooka stuck to his vegetarian guns, however. He informed the team that a diet based on meat added to the risk of injury, while a natural foods diet would protect them against sprains and dislocations. He further told them that a natural foods diet without meat would increase their *mental* energy and thus lead them to peak performance on the playing field. Now everybody, especially the media and other teams in the Pacific League, was roaring with laughter at the seemingly absurd Lions. One team, the Nippon-Ham Fighters was actually sponsored by a big meat company. That team manager ridiculed the Lions by calling them "weed eaters," and scorned them as being "the goat team."

Yes, they all made fun of the "goat team," but, as the saying goes, they laughed all the way to the bank. Amazingly, fortified with their new diet, the Lions zoomed from last place to first place. And whom did they have to fight for the Pacific League Crown? You've got it—none other than the Nippon-Ham Fighters. It was Armaged on, the final clash of the Titans, (the Vegetarians versus the Meat Eaters). And who won? Naturally, the natural food vegetarian Lions won. The Lions were unstoppable. They next defeated the Chunichi Dragons, glorifying themselves as the Japanese series winners. People were not laughing at the Lions anymore. In fact, the vegetarian Lions won kudos as being the nation's best baseball team. And to prove this was not merely chance, a freak vegetarian "hurricane," the Lions encored the following year in 1983 to once again triumph as league and national champions.

The media have provided us with accounts of people turning the tide against such terrible afflictions as cancer with the adoption of a macrobiotic, brown rice and grain based diet. And, now we see that such a diet can turn the tide in the direction of victory in sports. People working in the East-West Foundation, macrobiotic centers, insist that a carefully worked out natural foods diet can definitely improve athletic performance. It has been found that whole grains and various natural foods can, indeed, increase endurance and stamina for the athlete. In particular, long distance runners have benefited from macrobiotic programs of eating. Such a natural foods diet is also helpful for maintaining strength in the sport of baseball.

Phillip Kushi, the director of the East-West Foundation in Brookline, Massachusetts, and the son of Michio Kushi, the world's foremost authority in the field of macrobiotics, claims that a specific and appropriate macrobiotic diet can be worked out for each specific sport. For example, if a weight lifter was relying upon a macrobiotic diet, more protein would be included in his program to provide energy for the short thrusts of power required.

What we have been reviewing in the world of sports is actually revolutionary, the emergence of a whole new lifestyle, an entirely new way of looking at how to train for sports. Perhaps, the center of this new view of the sporting world consists in the awareness of the significance of the role of mind and the use of mind games in athletic games.

Rick Honeycutt was having a hard time—two straight defeats. What do you do with a baseball player who is experiencing trouble with his game? Call someone in to help him improve his techniques? No! This is what happened: "while shagging fly balls with other Los Angeles Dodgers pitchers, Honeycutt approached teammate Matt Young and asked for the phone number of Young's psychologist, Saul Miller."[4] Honeycutt has concluded "much of the game is mental." Yogi Berra has made the same point, and Jerry Sullivan comments, "psychologists are beginning to make headway in the mainstream of American sport."[5] Look what has been happening:

- American Psychological Association has a new division
- Exercise and Sports Psychology
- Higher education is offering sports psychology courses
- Major League Baseball teams are hiring consulting psychologists
- Olympic training centers have full-time psychologists
- National Football and Basketball are going into counseling

While a new importance of mind has found its way into sports, a new way of understanding the body has also emerged—one emphasizing its inherent wisdom. The major shift in understanding, which has resulted from new philosophies of mind and body, places emphasis not upon ox like physical strength, rigidity or big muscles, but upon fluidity, flexibility, dynamic energy, mobility. Consistent with the new view of mind and body is a new view of eating. The old stuff about stuffing on steak and maximizing protein is being replaced by the realization of the need for more simple diets that provide energy rather than brute power.

One of the most interesting programs in keeping with the new approach is Dr. Robert Haas's sports nutrition bible. His best-selling book is called *Eat To Win*. One of the myths about food for athletes that Haas strikes down is that protein is needed for top performance in sports. The old "steak and eggs" diet is now going out. Athletss consume as much as eight times more protein than they require each day. All the protein one needs per day is 40 to 80 grams—probably about five times less than one actually gets.

Enzymes and acids digest protein into amino acids, and then protein can be absorbed into the blood where it is used to repair cells and tissues and to fortify the immune system and keep the body operating in many ways. The more protein one takes in is not used to do more useful work on the body. After protein does its basic work it is converted into fat and sugar. The result is that excess protein does not mean more muscles but more fat.

Protein metabolism releases toxic waste products into the body which culminate in *urea*, and thus too much protein, or more than 80 grams, places a strain on the liver and kidneys which have to cleanse the body of these potential poisons. In this process of trying to cleanse, vital minerals, potassium, calcium and magnesium are lost. The added protein instead of serving the body can dehydrate it. Thus the athlete trying to build himself up by consuming extra protein is actually breaking himself down. The body simply cannot store extra protein, and thus we are simply endangering the body by using more than 80 grams of protein. When more than 80 grams of protein is eaten *putrefaction* of the excess occurs in the colon. Dr. Alice Chase asserts, "Chronic disease in many forms may be found in people whose colons are chronically stagnant cess-pools because of excessive protein eating."[6] Athletes have consumed generous amounts of meat that develop power. Meat protein may be the most dangerous, however. This is so because meat products decompose in the digestive tract, where they can become toxic.

Prolonged use of meat results in an accumulation in the tissues and vital organs of toxic dead animal wastes. These have a degenerative effect on the body, and thus instead of serving the athlete, deenergizes him or her.

Another false piece of conventional wisdom concerning nutrition for athletes is that they need salt tablets. Many coaches and trainers did have athletes on salt tablets. Salt tablets are counterproductive. They take away from the muscles. By taking away from the body, salt tablets can lead to dehydration.

Another danger for athletes can occur in what they drink. Nutritionist expert Dr. Haas tells of a drink that was especially developed by an expert on physiology and athletics. The drink contained saccharin, sugar, salts and water. The point of the formula was to provide the athletes with something that would get into their bloodstream more rapidly than water and thus give them a fix of quick calories. This is a very famous sports drink. Athletes *go for it* in a big way. What is the truth? It has been scientifically demonstrated that plain *water* gets into the bloodstream much quicker than the famous sports drink. Not only can't you fool Mother Nature, but it is rather hard to improve on her. Plain water is a wonderful drink.

Water is certainly more valuable to the athlete than *beer*. Beer is another "no, no" on the list of Dr. Haas. It was believed that athletes should consume beer after a competition to replace fluid that was lost during competition. The truth is, however, that alcohol is a dehydrating substance. Alcohol blocks the release of a hormone called ADH. This is not good because the function of ADH is to regulate the amount of water lost in urine. Thus if the pituitary gland cannot release enough ADH, the result is the loss of much needed water. Of course, beer or any other form of alcohol is harmful to the liver and kidneys, and it destroy vitamins.

Thus for the athlete the popular old nutritional script has

to be rewritten. Protein, steaks, eggs, salt, and beer can deenergize rather than energize.

Contrary to what had once been believed, carbohydrates are vital to the athlete. We know that exercise can lower blood sugar. The consequence is that the athlete may feel shaky, fatigued, and lightheaded. This condition cannot be helped by eating more protein. High-protein foods are often high-fat foods. The brain that is not getting enough sugar should not have protein nor fat. What is indicated is the complex carbohydrate. We are talking about brown rice again or pasta, whole grain cereals or breads. These kinds of foods supply the blood with sugar at the right rate, not too fast nor too slow. Complex carbohydrates are a clean burning and readily available source of blood sugar. It is reported that:

> "Mary Decker, a world class half miler at age fourteen, would insist on a plate of plain spaghetti three hours before a race. At the time, everyone thought that she was strange," remarks Brooks Johnson, former U.S. Olympic track coach. "Now runners realize that spaghetti is loaded with carbohydrates."[7]

Carbohydrates provide the body with energy more efficiently, quicker than fats. They are digested and absorbed faster into the bloodstream. Thus not only the stomach but the muscles too will get the blood, which is important for the athlete.

Thus since, as we have seen, carbohydrates are essential to athletic performance, it certainly follows that the "no-carbohydrates" diet that athletes, particularly bodybuilders, have been experimenting with is worse than useless. The premise of the "no-carbohydrate" diet was that eliminating foods containing carbohydrates would get rid of fat while at the same time permitting muscle growth. Unfortunately that is not the way it works. Along with the loss of fat a "no-carbohydrate" diet causes loss of *muscle tissue*. The fact is that the body must have carbohydrates in order to metabolize protein. What happens when carbohydrates are cut out is that muscles cannot use protein for its functions.

It is clear that the master athlete should not cut out carbohydrates, but he might safely cut out coffee. Athletes drink coffee because it contains something that gives them stimulation—*caffeine*. The trouble is that caffeine also over stimulates the nervous system. In addition it has a diuretic function which can lead to dehydration of the body. This diuretic effect of caffeine is also irritating to the kidneys.

In addition to the high caffeine content in coffee, tea, cocoa, and cola, soft drinks alos contain undesirable levels of caffeine. Cocoa has not as much caffeine as coffee, of course, but it has another stimulant, theobromine, harmfully increasing the addictive quantity of chemicals. As for the cola soft drinks, they not only have caffeine but chemical additives and white sugar. And that brings us to another hazard for the athlete and anyone who wishes to be healthy.

Sugar is appealing to many as a quick energy fix. Unfortunately, the fix will not fix your energy needs for long, and then there will follow a letdown. Sugar does not possess anything that could possibly do one any good. It has no vitamins, no minerals, no protein. The only thing sugar has going for it is that it tastes good, and that is bad because it creates a desire for something one should not be putting into his or her system. Sugar—and this is also true of refined flour—adversely affects the metabolism of the body by supplying energy to the body without the nutrition the body requires for functioning.

It is the case that sugar provides quick energy. It does so by raising the blood sugar level for a short period after which it abruptly falls. In about 30 minutes the sugar is depleted, and aftereffects may be fatigue, headache, dizziness and irritability.

Refined white flour poses severe problems for all of us and certainly the athlete. Commercial white bread is filled with chemicals, emptied of nutrition, and then injected with an emulsifier to make it soft. After all this, it is given some synthetic vitamins and called *enriched*. It has to be enriched in the second place because it has been so impoverished in the first place. To produce white bread a perfectly healthful wheatberry is savaged. The wheat germ is discarded and many of the vitamins as well as proteins are lost while the starch is kept. One reason white flour is used rather than wheat is that it has a much longer shelf life. Bugs even avoid bleached flour because it cannot nourish them. In an experiment at Rochester University one group of rats was fed "enriched" white bread and another was fed unbleached natural wheat bread. The rats fed the natural bread developed and procreated in a very healthy way. The rats who got the white bread became sickly and didn't last long. In another test Dr. Williams reported of mice dying from malnutrition as a result of being only fed bread made of refined flour. The athlete who seeks energy, stamina and endurance, then, must be wary of not only alcohol but coffee, tea, cola soft drinks, white sugar, and flour. It is also wise to cut back on protein, and cut down on meats.

Beyond McDonalds and Dunkin Donuts

Once upon a time animals lived out in the open and fed on grasses and whole grains. For meat eaters they did not pose the health problems that animals consumed today do. Now the *factory farm* has succeeded the *family farm*, and animals are forced to live in crammed, filthy, germ-ridden pens. They are fed starchy low-protein grains and shot up with chemicals and hormones to make them fat. They are treated so horribly their nerves are worked up, and they therefore are also tranquilized. Livestock are also loaded up with antibiotics. When so many *antibiotics* are administered, a resistance is developed, and then they cannot do the one job they are designed to do, namely give us protection. Further, the drugs kill bacteria indiscriminately, not just bad or toxic bacteria but good bacteria that helps us fight disease. As for pork products, Gary and Stephen Null warn:

> After a short life spent in a crowded environment, eating processed garbage, the pig is subjected to a final insult before slaughter. Sodium pentobarbital, a powerful anesthetic, is injected into its blood stream to relax its muscles, so that the flesh will be redder and more tender.[8]

It has been commented that the pig is a sick animal when sent to market and would die long before its time if we did not rush it out so that humans could feast on it.

In the ancient world when the philosopher Diogenes was asked what he thought of athletes, he responded that they are "nothing but beef and pork." Today that will certainly not be true of the master athlete. For the master athlete in our age realizes the necessity of keeping the mind, the spirit, and the body in shape. He will not only understand the importance of the mind in sports, but of the natural wisdom of the body and of a more natural approach to food.

It is amazing how all things come together. There is a consistent style in today's approach to training through the mind, exercising the body, and in eating. We may actually conclude that a revolutionary philosophy has arisen which has given athletes, women and men, a new way of using their minds, their bodies, and of eating.

This revolutionary philosophy is consistent with a great shift in our model of the cosmos from the Newtonian to the post-Einstein or quantum era. Whereas reality in the Newtonian view was solid, massive, static, and understood in terms of the category of *substance*, in the view after Einstein's theory of relativity and quantum mechanics, it is viewed in terms of *energy* and *process*, and is more dynamic. One can see the same change in understanding sports: massive physical power and substance is no longer central. Dynamic energy and flexible mobility are now more at the core of athletic prowess. It is more the model based on the skill of a Muhammad Ali than the physical strength of a John L. Sullivan. With regard to nutrition, this means eating more naturally and simply. There should be less emphasis on protein, on meat, milk and eggs, and more emphasis on brown rice, grains, vegetables, fruit and nuts. As we have seen, carbohydrates such as pasta and potatoes are fine for today's athlete. The question may arise as to whether the athlete can get adequate energy from diet alone or whether there should be an addition of supplements.

Beyond McDonalds and Dunkin Donuts

In our polluted world in which pure air and water are nowhere to be found and in which there is so much stress, vitamin and mineral supplements, contrary to what many doctors and dietitians tell us, may be essential for healthful living. This is all the more true for peak performance in sports. This brings us to a discussion of the value of vitamins and supplements for the athlete.

WHAT YOU ALWAYS WANTED TO KNOW ABOUT VITAMINS

But Your Doctor was Afraid You Would Ask

Sports medicine authorities Dr. Gabe Mirkin and Marshall Hoffman categorically assert, "I now know what nutritionists have known for decades: Everything your body needs can be supplied by a proper diet."[1] This statement echoes the medical establishment's party line. It is simply not true that we can get all we need from what we eat. Our sports medicine authorities use the expression *proper* diet. That is a bit tricky. By *proper* diet we refer to one that will provide us with all the nutrition we need. One of the qualities of the overpolluted and poisoned environment we dwell in—with the contaminated and chemically saturated food we eat in our high-tech, very high-stress world—is precisely that we no longer get a *proper* diet. While no one wants to encourage irresponsible vitamin popping, still it must be recognized supplements may be necessary. It is important for the athlete to understand this.

Linus Pauling, the eminent scientist and Nobel Prize recipient, who has so thoroughly investigated and researched Vitamin C for over 15 years, makes it rather clear that the advice of the medical establishment concerning vitamins is not very nourishing:[2]

> I am a scientist, a chemist, physicist, crystallographer, molecular biologist and medical researcher. Twenty years ago I became interested in the vitamins. I discovered that the science of nutrition had stopped developing. The old professors of nutrition who had helped develop this science fifty years ago seemed to so sell satisfied with their accomplishment that they ignored the new discoveries that were being made in biochemistry, molecular biology and medicine, including vitamins and other nutrients. [3]

The medical establishment did not keep up with—or ignored—this important research. Dr. Pauling is right on target: "Although a new science of nutrition was being developed, these old professors of nutrition continued to teach their students the old ideas, many of them wrong, such as that no person in ordinary health needs to take supplementary vitamins and that all you need to do for good nutrition is to eat some of each of the `four foods' each day."[3] Logically, Pauling draws the conclusion from this that many nutritionists and dietitians today are still practicing the *old* nutrition, and this results in the fact that "the American people are not as healthy as they should be." Pauling also points out that physicians are also guilty, because most of them have only received a small amount of nutrition in medical school, and much of that was out of date, anyhow.

Unfortunately the medical profession to a large degree is not involved in *making people healthy*, but rather in treating disease. That is fine, and many are dedicated to doing so, however, making people healthy might mean we could *prevent* disease. Often when doctors get around to *treating* it, it is too late anyhow. Of course, the athlete wants to be in top health, and that worthy goal can be served by a judicious use of supplements.

We should not forget that for years the medical establishment refused to recognize the significance of eating the right food to prevent cancer. It finally reached the point that no one could deny the crucial relevance of diet in relation to such terrible afflictions as cancer. Leonard A. Cohen in an informative article in *Scientific American* reports:

> In 1982 the National Research Council ... issued provisional guidelines intended to reduce the risk of cancer related to food. The main recommendations were to lower the intake of fat from the current U.S. average of 40 percent of total calories to 30 percent; to eat more fiber, fruits and vegetables; to increase the consumption of complex carbohydrates (such as the starch in

flour and potatoes), and to decrease the consumption of pickled, salted or smoked foods as well as of simple carbohydrates (such as refined sugar).[4]

What is revealing is that exactly the type of nutritional guidelines issued to reduce the risk of cancer apply to the kind of foods achieving-athletes should be getting. It is most consistent with our discussion in the preceding chapter.

What is really important to understand, and what Leonard A. Cohen emphasizes, is that human diet has undergone drastic change in a short time span when considered agains the backdrop of evolution. Studying hunter-gatherer societies that still exist in the 20th century, such as the Bushmen of the Kalahari desert in Southern Africa, throws light on questions about natural diet. The fat intake of prehistoric people living in temperate climates was about 20 percent of total calories. That is half of what we consume in the United States. Further, prehistoric people had a much higher ratio of unsaturated to saturated fat. Their fiber intake was about 45 grams a day, while ours in the U.S. is about 15 grams or less. And their intake of ascorbic acid was four times more than ours.

It turns out that for more than 90 percent of human history people have survived on low-fat, high-fiber diets with high levels of ascorbic acid and calcium. What this means is that today's people are going about with metabolic and digestive systems that were evolved to eat very differently than we are now eating. Evolution did not design us to eat the way we do. This is related to why we get sick with obesity, heart diseases and cancers that were not common in earlier periods of history.

Leonard A. Cohen notes, "At present, several factors are seen as tumor promoters or anti-promoters. The item most clearly established as a promoter is dietary fat. The possible anti-promoters include dietary fiber; vitamins A, C and E; the trace element selenium, and certain compounds in such vegetables as broccoli, cabbage and cauliflower, which are called cruciferous vegetables."[5] These may detoxify. The point is that what we are eating now may be so at variance with what we were basically built to metabolize and digest that we must supplement with vitamins such as A, B, C and E, and with minerals such as magnesium and calcium, and trace minerals such as selenium.

Nutritionist expert Jane E. Brody informs us that "heavy meat-eating by modern affluent societies may be exceeding the biological capacities evolution built into the human body."[6] The point is that we need supplements because it so difficult for us to get that proper diet the medical experts praise. The nutritionist expert, Dr. Paavo Airola, says that, perhaps, one might have been able to get it 100 years ago, but not now.

According to Dr. Airola, "today when soils are depleted, when foods are loaded with residues of hundreds of toxic insecticides and other chemicals, and when the nutritional value of virtually all food is drastically lowered by vitamin, protein, and enzyme-destroying practices (such as harvesting the produce before it is ripe), the addition of vitamins and food supplements to the diet is of vital importance."[7]

It should be clear that diet alone is not sufficient, and therefore I will not burden you further with many more technical details that could be added in support of using supplements. I will just say that it is the case that vitamin and mineral supplements can be beneficial to most people, and in particular they may be highly beneficial to athletes.

Certainly the problem of *free radicals* makes vitamin and mineral supplementation very important. Environmental sickness is a most serious problem in our industrial civilization. Toxic chemicals taken in one's body are converted by enzymes into a new molecular form called *free radicals*. Free radicals have been identified as the cause of environmental sickness and of cancer. A free radical is a molecule that has an additional electron that is not paired with any other electron. Electrons paired together have stability. Free radicals are extremely unstable, and their additional electrons seek stability by joining with another cell. What is called *oxidation* occurs when a free radical finds an electron and yanks it away from the cell it was in. Oxidation is bad because it causes cell damage. Pollution, additives, and various chemicals increase the production of free radicals.

Vitamins A, C and E, minerals such as manganese and zinc, the trace mineral selenium and beta carotene so function as to stop free radicals from joining with cell components, and thereby prevent the cell from being damaged.

Actually, problems of pollution are magnified for the athlete. The athlete has to work out in the polluted environment, and in doing so ingests more poisons than the sedentary individual. *Lecithin* and *kelp* are supplements which would be helpful here, for they neutralize bodily poisons. Pure spring water and plenty of raw foods are also indicated. Amino acids, taurine and cystine are also useful for people who are especially vulnerable to the attack of pollutants.

In an article on "Nutrition And The Athlete," Neva Jensen observes that the quick energy snack foods the athlete often relies upon have negative consequences such as obesity, and that nonnutritive stimulants such as carbonated drinks cannot support good energy metabolism.

Neva Jensen asserts, "Nutritional needs of the athlete should be of prime concern in maintaining a healthy heart and good circulation, as well as providing cellular nutrition to every part of the body."[8] She advises powdered protein drinks *if* they are consumed slowly and contain minerals, enzymes and unsaturated oils. Indian runners used seeds such as flax, chia, sesame, sunflower, and pumpkin to get stamina and endurance.

Neva Jensen's research also turns up the information that *kelp*, a common seaweed, due to its mineral and iodine content helps the thyroid gland in controlling and regulating the burning of fats which are the body's most consistent form of energy. *Kelp* normalizes the thyroid and the secretion of thyroxin to bring vitality to muscle cells.

Cayenne is recommended for circulation. Heartbeat increases with vigorous exercise, and cayenne helps here by enabling the tissue to receive more blood. Cayenne also promotes elasticity and tone in blood vessels.

Ginger assists digestive functions, while *peppermint*, by stimulating gastric flow, makes possible better utilization of food nutrients. Supplementation by herbs can thus benefit circulation and glandular functioning.

Gayle Olinekova, an athlete, who wrote a book called *Go For It!* reminds us of the value of *garlic*. Appreciation of the worth of garlic goes back as far as the time of Hercules. He believed his strength was derived from a clove of garlic he wore about his neck. Nutritional research has now established that garlic is an antioxidant, and antiviral aid and has the capacity to help removing fats from the blood.

In his book, *Miracle Medical Foods*, Rex Adams announces that scientists have discovered an amazing healing plant that can relieve prostate trouble, high blood pressure, heart symptoms, diabetes, can help lower cholesterol, and can help ease arthritis, and soothe the stomach and aid digestion. What is nature's all-purpose miracle remedy? Believe it or not, it is *garlic*. Two substances isolated in it are particularly effective in making us healthy and in fighting germs and disease. They are *alliin* and *alicin*. Researchers have further isolated the vital trace minerals selenium and germanium.

No less valuable for the athlete than the amazing garlic is the amazing *ginseng*. It has been well-founded that ginseng increases *endurance* and *stamina*. Further, it is beneficial for circulation, the heart and digestion, and relieves stress. A Japanese researcher, Keijiro Takagi, reports ginseng has antifatigue properties. Frances Sheridan Goulart says, "For the athlete, ginseng's greatest value is as an endurance booster and a non-exciting stimulant."[9] It is important to know that ginseng is not a drug. It is classed as an *adaptogen*. Adaptogens normalize body functions.

The word *adaptogen* was coined by a Russian scientist, N.V. Lazarev, who defined it as a nontoxic substance that provides us with resistance to various types of stress. Dr. Betty Kamen explains that while a drug only relieves symptoms, an adaptogen works on a cellular level and deals with root causes.[10]

Siberian ginseng which was the basis for the adaption of the term improves functioning of the adrenal glands, and in doing so helps relieve stress.

What You Always Wanted to Know About Vitamins

In Switzerland's Consultox Laboratories it was found that mice given ginseng show an increase in stamina and endurance in swimming tests up to 60 percent. A distinguished Russian scientist, Dr. I.I. Brekham, reported that daily doses of ginseng increased physical endurance and mental capacity for work. Frances Sheridan Goulart says, according to Breckham's research, "ginseng does three things of paramount importance to anyone in the thick or thin of athletics: it affects the function of the blood system, increases muscle tone, and stabilizes carbohydrate metabolism. As a result of these and other findings, ginseng is now as much a staple in the diets of Russian Olympic athletes."[11]

It is valuable to take ginseng in conjunction with the Oriental herb, *gota kola*. *Gota kola* is well known for its *rejuvenating* properties. It is said that gota kola energizes cells of the brain.

Ginseng and gota kola might be reinforced with *ephedra*, a desert herb that when used with B vitamins and cayenne stimulates the entire central nervous system.

Another source of high energy is *bee pollen*. It was used for increasing energy as far back as the ancient Greek Olympics. Bee pollen gives energy and endurance. A former Russian Olympic coach conducted a two- year research study of bee pollen, and confirmed bee pollen improves recovery power in athletes. His research project was centered in Pratt Institute in New York. He found users of bee pollen regained energy faster, and got better on second and third efforts even after intense exertion.

Dr. Susan Smith Jones comments that an athlete trained on bee pollen will stabilize his body functions more quickly than someone who uses steroids to achieve artificial musculature and short-lived prowess. "Recuperation of ATP (adenoisine triphosphate which governs energy) occurred faster with athletes who had taken bee pollen."[12]

It has been over 60 years now that researchers have been trying to find just what it is in wheat germ that has been providing athletes with so excellent a source of energy. It was thought to be vitamin E which amply occurs in wheat germ oil. It has finally been found to be something else—*octacosanol*, an octacosyl alcohol. It is found in alfalfa, vegetable oils, and in its highest concentration in wheat germ oil.

Octacosanol definitely has been found to improve stamina, endurance and reflex-reaction time. It can regenerate nerves. Octacosonal helps tremendously in heavy training or intense exercise. Octacosonal can be regarded as a super energy source.

Carlson Wade, nutrition expert, informs us:

> "the wheat germ oil concentrate remains the only clinically proven substance that increases exercise tolerance, reduces blood cholesterol, improves oxygen utilization and acts as a neuromuscular factor to prohibit muscle pain after exercise. It also improves reaction time and reduces stress at high altitudes, a boon to mountain climbers."[13]

Dr. Richard Passwater asserts, "The favorable physiological responses thus far attributable to octacosanol include increased stamina, endurance and vigor. Basal metabolism, oxygen utilization, reaction time and nerve function are also significantly improved."[14]

What You Always Wanted to Know About Vitamins

There are endless possibilities in terms of supplements for the athlete, and certainly an outstanding one is vitamin B-15 which has been demonstrated to improve oxygen metabolism and eliminate "anoxia" or oxygen starvation in body cells and tissues. It normalizes fat metabolism and sugar metabolism. B-15 is enhanced when used in conjunction with vitamins A and E. It is not approved in our country.[15] It is ironic that America historically was the land people escaped from tyranny to come to in order to enjoy freedom of choice, and now, in regard to so many health and nutrition options, people must escape from America to attain freedom of choice.

Despite what establishment nutritionists and physicians say there can be no doubt that what Dr. Richard You, the U.S. Olympic Games 1977 team physician, claimed is true, that being that vitamins can spell the difference between a champion and an also-ran. Further, he observed that most athletes are at times affected by nutritional deficiencies.

The athlete can enhance his performance and keep well and fit using beta carotene, a B-complex formula, vitamin C, vitamin D, vitamin E, vitamin P or bioflavonoids, lecithin, brewer's yeast, the trace mineral selenium, SOD, or superoxide dismutase, a multi-mineral capsule, garlic, ginseng, gota kola, bee pollen, octacosonal, and if available B-15.

To round it out, one should not simply eat, but eat simply and naturally, consuming properly cooked vegetables, raw fruits, vegetables and nuts and much fiber, whole grains and natural breads, complex carbohydrates, not carbohydrates like white sugar. One should cut down on protein, meats, and carbonated drinks. Raw juices and pure water may not be what the doctor ordered, but they are what nature ordered.

LOSING TO WIN

The Need to Win over Your Own Needs

In the hit Broadway play *Damn Yankees* the hero sells his soul to the devil to become a great baseball star. It is tragic but true. Athletes will sell out to the devil. In *The Sports Medicine Book* we read, "A few years ago I polled more than a hundred top runners and posed this question: If I could give you a pill that would make you an Olympic champion—and also kill you in a year—would you take it? To my amazement more than half of the athletes responding stated that they would take my magic pill.[1] The authors of *The Sports Medicine Book* claim that drug-taking is a monumental problem. The unfortunate irony is that stimulants definitely do not improve athletic performance. Learning this can be a fatally costly lesson. Thus, as far back as 1890, a British cyclist died while racing due to a stimulant, *ephedrine*, which he had taken. Of course, today what is frightening is that drug usage is so extensive that the problem is out of control.

That in fact is the title of Hollywood Henderson's book about his drug abuse. Thomas "Hollywood" Henderson revealed in his autobiography *Out of Control* that he took drugs while playing for four different teams and went so far as to sniff a cocaine-laced inhaler during Super Bowl XIII. At Super Bowl XIII, played against the Steelers in 1978, Thomas Henderson in his book with co-author Peter Knobler tells us that he put one and a half grams of cocaine into an inhaler and mixed it with water.

Henderson said that he knew he was going to get banged around and his nose was going to hurt. So, he claimed that in addition to his addiction he wanted cocaine as a "medication," to "anesthetize" his face. Then in the second half of the Orange Bowl with 80,000 screaming fans and another 200 million watching on TV, Henderson was right there on the sideline snorting coke. He said his team lost that day, he lost that day. He was "out of control."

It is sad and truly frightening that the drug problem has leaped so out of control, because it transforms what sports are all about. It takes the true spirit of spontaneous play out of sport, which can be a beautiful thing to behold, and it turns it into something ugly, a destructive drive to win that dooms the athlete such as Henderson to becoming a loser. It is also disturbing because it is true as the title of a book by Robert H. Boyle puts it: Sport: *Mirror of American Life*. It is a tragic, vicious cycle, because our way of life with its loss of values spills into sports and contaminates them; sports as a model for behavior and athletes as role models reflect their problems back to masses of sports fans.

The drug problem has become so terrible and so overwhelming that it is spawning a new class of super wealthy. In an article called "Drug Business," Nicholas Pileggi reports that dope is New York's hottest cash business. Illegal drug dealers do such big business and accumulate such fabulous profits that one of their problems, explained lawyer Edward Hayes, is that they forget where they put their money. One dealer simply forgot where he buried $300,000 in upstate New York and another hid some in a basement closet and, when he went to get it, discovered mice had already come and eaten about $50,000 worth.[2] In a new book by Mark Bowden called *Doctor Dealer*, we learn that a sophisticated Main Line dentist built up a $60 million a year drug empire. The point is that Larry Lavin, the Main Line dentist was arrested in Virginia Beach, Virginia, in May of 1986 and is going to spend the next 42 years of his life in prison. Drugs ruined his life just as they almost ruined the life of Hollywood Henderson.

We may conclude that the extensive use of drugs is ruining our society. We must overcome this terrible social burden, and the athlete must overcome getting caught in the drug trap. In the program I have been talking about, for one to become a master or ultimate athlete there can be no place for drugs. The new philosophy, which we feel must become the premise of peak performance in sports, is a way of returning us to the center of ourselves through philosophy, zen, meditation, visualization, getting in harmony with the natural rhythm of our bodies through natural eating and a simple way of life. In following such a philosophy the athlete cannot only clean up his own act and excel in sports, but can contribute to social problems by becoming a positive role model.

Much drug use by athletes, of course, is not for thrills or selfish pleasure, but as a means seen to assist sports performance. It does not work, but athletes are very much involved in "doing drugs" to help them with sporting problems, and drugs are very much doing bad things to athletes.

Athletes take *uppers*, stimulants to help them overcome fatigue and to lose weight, and they take *downers* to help them deal with the *manic* feelings they get from taking *uppers*. After using *uppers* they may have a difficult time getting to sleep or calming down, and so they go to *barbiturates*, downers, intoxicant drugs such as Luminal, Seconal, or Nembutal. These depress the sleep-center nerves. The result is that athletes get caught in a dizzying revolving door. They have fatigue, and so get high and speed up on amphetamines, and then need to slow down, and thus get low on downers, and then return to uppers to speed up again. It's a trap that leads nowhere.

The other class of drugs relied on extensively by athletes are *anabolic steroids*. It is thought that these can help the body heal itself and can give strength. The anabolic steroids are called "Rambo drugs," because they build up muscle and get you going. A sports medicine doctor on the Olympic committee, Dr. Robert Voy, talked about the Charles Atlas syndrome. Young people are starting to take steroids to be able to show off muscles. Steroids have become so popular for muscle builders, bodybuilders, football players or anyone else wanting to develop strength that we are told drug dealers "sold an estimated $100 million in black market steroids" in 1986 alone.[3]

Despite the widespread use among athletes of steroids, they have terrible side effects. Mirkin and Hoffman note that side effects include dizziness, sterility, sexual problems, headaches, hostility and aggressiveness, intestinal bleeding, liver disease, and cancer.

Gladys Portugues, who is a well-known first class professional bodybuilder, has estimated that of the top 30 female bodybuilders, about 20 are probably steroid users, and many of them are heavy users.

Tina Plakinger was a bodybuilder who used steroids right from the start. She said they allowed her to get bigger and stronger at an amazing rate. She won 11 bodybuilding titles. In 1982 Tina won the Ms. America title, the top amateur bodybuilding contest in the world.

Tina Plakinger was getting what she wanted in becoming a winner in contests all over the world, but she was getting other things she did not want, such as hair on her face, and her voice was becoming so low she was often mistaken for a man on the phone. She confessed, "I went from being a very soft, fawn-like creature to becoming a raging bull." She elaborates, "One night my husband was late for dinner. When he finally walked through the door, I was so enraged that I threw him against the door and held him there. He couldn't move, he was so shocked. I'll tell you, living with me on steroids was no day at the beach."[4]

David Groves, who researched the problem, explains why there are strong reasons against using steroids. Testosterone, a hormone required to build muscle, exists in large quantities in men and only in minute quantities in women. Testosterone is responsible for changes that take place in males during puberty. These include lower voice, growth of body hair, broad shoulders, development of male sex drive and aggressiveness.

Anabolic steroids are examples of testosterone manufactured in the laboratory. They were first used to treat people with medical problems. Today they are almost never so used.

Their use now is in connection with bodybuilding. Athletes combine different kinds of steroids and take them in massive doses, which can be quite dangerous. Men as well as women experience disturbing side effects. As a result of using anabolic steroids male athletes may find a decrease in the size of their testicles, a reduction in sperm count, balding, growth of breasts, and an increase in hostility. Both sexes may develop liver disorders and cardiovascular problems. There are cases of steroid users becoming psychotic

As dangerous or more so than the steroids are amphetamines, or *uppers*. Amphetamines are taken to boost performance. Their getting one high is short-lived. Again, it is selling one's soul to the devil. Dick Howard, a 1960 Olympic medalist, experimented with amphetamines to make himself tops in going over the hurdles. As he took more of the drug, however, he could not get over the hurdles of life, and ended up a year later dying of an overdose.

Amphetamines cause users to be less sensitive to pain; and therefore, one on an upper may be unable to realize how badly he is hurt and thus will not stop an athletic effort when in danger. A runner on amphetamines may die from heart stroke, as a result of pushing too hard and going too far.

Amphetamines also cloud judgment, causing athletes to think they are doing better than they are. One pitcher on amphetamines thought he was getting everybody out with his pitching when in fact the batters were knocking his pitches all over the lot.

Amphetamines give a sense of well-being, are good for dieters because they frustrate feelings of being hungry, they mask fatigue, and give rise to illusions of athletic grandeur, letting the athlete feel there is no limit to his energy and strength. Some of the main amphetamines are Henzedrine, Dexedrine, and Methylamphetamine.

These drugs do the same kind of things to our body that cocaine does. In fact cocaine and the amphetamines produce the release of *norepinephrine*, a hormone from the brain, and prevent its return to storage sites. After a short period, stronger and stronger doses are required. Amphetamines cause so powerful an effect on the emotions, that when they are stopped *depression* sets in. Amphetamines, the uppers, also cause sleep loss, paranoia, and loss of memory.

Pat Croce, who worked with the Philadelphia Flyers and is currently president of the Philadelphia 76'ers, has some interesting comments concerning drug use. As a psychotherapist, I must say his view is good psychology. In a column on "Personal Fitness" in *The Philadelphia Inquirer*, Pat Croce warns of the dangers of steroid use, but his criticism is perfectly applicable to the use of uppers and downers as well. Pat Croce notes that, having trained some of the best professional athletes alive such as Julius Erving, Mike Schmidt and Bobby Clarke, he knows that a person does not have to take steroids, and he would add, drugs of any kind, to be a winner. He says that these world-class athletes he has trained are living proof that a dedicated individual can reach the top in sports "without resorting to any harmful additives." Drugs give us only harmful illusions, but Pat Croce observes, "It is possible to achieve this same strength with proper training, nutrition and commitment, and it is a heck of a lot safer."[6]

This is precisely the understanding that I have been developing in this book. It is not only possible but necessary to achieve excellence in sports, to develop the spirit, mind, and body in a holistic, natural and simple way. There are no shortcuts, no magical formulas, nor are there any royal roads. Anything you must take that is *external* to you can be lost, and can become master to you. Thus if you rely on drugs and cannot obtain them, you feel frustrated and filled with anxiety. You want these "easy" means to live, but they do not work. You have got to work yourself, and only then have "you got it." To develop the mind through meditation, prayer, and concentration is to become strong within, and there is no need for drugs. To understand the messages your body is sending you through biofeedback, or a biorhythm chart, or by coming to understand the inner wisdom of your body, is to keep your body pure. If you treat your body properly, it will not crave drugs. And, of course, an important part of that is through good nutrition and the use of vitamins, minerals and herbs as food not as drugs. There must be a *positive* outlook. There has thus to be an optimistic philosophy of life. This is why the athlete requires mental training as well as physical training and good nutrition.

Even if an athlete is on drugs, it is possible to get off. Believe it or not, the first step, and the most difficult one is to *want* to get off. If one puts his mind and heart to any goal, and then works toward it, he can do it! One medical doctor who only accepted *terminal* cases of disease said that so long as a patient had *hope*, he knew a cure was possible. The athlete using drugs to excel must come to see that he or she is selling his or her soul to the devil, and then end the sale before eternal hell becomes a living reality. Once this is seen, many of the programs we have discussed can help bring the athlete out of hell, back toward heaven. It can happen.

People have gotten off drugs through religious programs, through meditation groups—TM people have often worked with drug abuse problems—through biofeedback programs, or through visualization. The point is that the techniques, the means, the methods are available. I have been reviewing them in this book, but the main responsibility lies with the individual. If he or she sincerely *desires* to change, then the program to do it will be found.

This does, of course, involve a changed way of viewing things. Once someone attains a *new way* of looking at a problem, new and vital energy becomes available to solve problems that previously may have seemed hopeless. This is why we have said that the athlete should not merely learn the new mental techniques and physical exercises, but should find a positive or affirmative philosophy to guide him. As Victor Frankl, who was incarcerated in a concentration camp, pointed out, in order to survive, we must have a *meaning* and a purpose. A philosophy of life provides that.

It is not facetious—even hockey players, basketball players, baseball players, or prizefighters need to believe in something. If you have a good set of beliefs, that will give confidence and thus feeling up, there will be more energy and better stamina and endurance. Plus, there will be great satisfaction that this comes from your mind rather than somebody else's drugs. On the other hand, if you do not really believe in anything, you will have no explanation for negative things that happen, and will feel down, and have less energy. People who are pessimistic easily get headaches and feel fatigued. Thus it is essential to believe the universe and life is good, and that you are part of that.

Harmonizing body, mind and spirit, and developing a positive philosophy is as relevant to other problems athletes develop, such as alcoholism and smoking, as it is to the use of amphetamines and steroids.

Alcohol is, of course, a dangerous drug, and is particularly harmful to athletes. There is the case of Norm Standlee. He was a powerhouse full back for Stanford in 1940. That was the team that made popular the T formation. Subsequently he played profootball for the Chicago Bears and San Francisco 49ers. He had everything going for him including a good family, good friends, and admiring fans. He blew it all, however, because of alcohol. He became an alcoholic, died alone and tragically in a motel. His alcohol habit caused him to suffer from cirrhosis of the liver. Ken Sprague in his book *The Athlete's Body* lists other victims to drink. They are wrestler Gorgeous George, baseball player Ryen Duren and basketball All-American Don Lofgran.

Don Newcombe found his baseball career coming to an abrupt ending due to too much booze. He could have gone on much longer if he had not succumbed to a drinking problem. Newcombe found he wasn't alone. There were many other athletes with the same problem. Newcombe, who went through a cure in an Arizona treatment center, became part of an alcohol rehabilitation program for the Los Angeles Dodgers.

Despite the terrible problems it gives rise to, alcohol has such universal appeal that all over the world it has been claimed to have been created by the gods. The Greeks venerated Dionysius, the guardian of the vine and the god of intoxication. In Rome, Dionysium became Bacchus, and drunkenness virtually became a religion. Someone said that Rome was one great saloon.

Alcohol is absorbed almost instantly, and thus there is no need to wait for its pleasures. It is not a stimulant, however, as some maintain. It is a narcotic. And performance is impaired by even small doses. Katherine Ketcham and Dr. Ann Mueller tell us, "Most alcoholics don't realize that alcohol, in addition to its direct, poisonous effects on organs such as the liver, heart, brain, and stomach, works indirectly as a sort of nutritional vacuum cleaner, sucking up vitamins and minerals and leaving the body with various deficiencies. Nutritional disorders are a devastating consequence of chronic alcoholism, for they literally affect every cell in the body, causing a wide array of mental and physical symptoms. Every drinking alcoholic is malnourished, meaning that many of his body cells are weakened, sick, or dying."[8]

When the person recognizes how bad things are getting, something can be done. It is a gigantic hurdle and a terrible struggle, but if the will is found there are ways. A very central way is nutrition. Roger Williams, a distinguished biochemist, has completed groundbreaking research into the problem of alcoholism, and sees nutrition as a powerful weapon to fight against it. It is necessary to eat the right kind of foods, to avoid the wrong kinds, to use vitamin and mineral supplements and to get exercise. Underlying all of this, one must take responsibility for oneself, for one's health, and for one's unique bodily needs.

The most frequent and yet most harmful error one caught up in drinking makes is to consume sweet things. Sweets actually provide an instant but very temporary relief. Sweets for the moment combat a depressed feeling, fatigue, and even desire for drink, but then they weaken sobriety to the point the alcoholic cannot fight against the need to drink. Sugar causes people with drinking problems to have blood sugar problems which can bring about a host of mental problems, including depression, hostility, and confusion. These can drive one back to drink.

Roger Williams thus advises avoidance of low quality foods such as refined flours, refined pastas, white bread, sugar, and caffeine. Follow a regular exercise program for the good of the circulatory system. Even athletes who get on heavy drink will get off regular exercise. Exercise is important, however, because it gives strength to the body and aids cells in resisting disease.

The diet for recovery should be based upon an understanding of the dangers of meat. In the first place meat protein is more difficult to digest than protein from vegetables, milk, cheese, nuts and grains. Since drinking is hard on the digestive system, the problem of digesting heavy loads of meat protein raises special difficulties for the alcoholic. Also, red meats are high in saturated fat, and this can lead to hardening of the arteries, high blood pressure and stroke. Meat protein has been linked with cancer of the colon.

What is good to eat for the athlete with a drinking problem are vegetables, grains, nuts and seeds, dairy products, and fruits. All vitamins are good, and especially the B vitamins, because they are destroyed by drinking. Minerals are also important for alcoholics. *Potassium* deficiencies are most common in alcoholics, and thus important to be supplemented. Alcohol also causes loss of much calcium, and calcium needs to be taken along with magnesium, which must be kept in balance with calcium and which is needed for the drinker's nerves and muscles. Lack of the trace mineral manganese can affect drinker's blood sugar control. Zinc is also valuable to an alcoholic because low levels of it are found in heavy drinkers with cirrhosis.

It is understandable that the late Adele Davis, nutrition authority, in her book *Let's Eat Right To Keep Fit* regards a good nutritional program and vitamin supplementation as the answer to alcoholism. In any case, it certainly helps.

The drinker who also smokes will be worse off, but if an athlete wants to do harm to himself, it is not necessary to drink; smoking can do enough harm on its own. Cigarette smoke contains carbon monoxide, and that lessens the oxygen carrying ability of the blood. Smoking also negatively affects the system of dust removal from the bronchial tubes of the lungs.

An anonymous author wrote *Counterbaste To Tobacco* in 1640, and described it as the *lively image and pattern of Hell*. According to that writer tobacco was attacked as hateful to eye and nose, and quite harmful to the brain and lungs. It turned out that the author of this was none other than James the First. He became King James and commissioned the King James Version of the Bible. King James detested Catholics, and just as the Pope, detested tobacco as well. But in the long run nothing could prevent the people from coming to love tobacco.

Eminent botanist Norman Taylor tells us that no plant in a brief period of 450 years has ever become so popular as tobacco. He points out that the tobacco habit stretched back as much as a thousand years before the first Spaniard arrived in the New World. In the New World, "Tobacco was the most widely used escape from fatigue, mental or physical, of the daily grind, far exceeding coca in this respect."[9]

Taylor further observes that little did the Indians realize that what they sought were the effects of one of the most poisonous alkaloids to be found in the world of plants, namely, *nicotine*. Nicotine in its pure form and in a lethal dose kills as fast as *cyanide*. Taylor comments, "What the Indians discovered in it were precisely the same narcotic effects which modern Americans crave to such an extent that in 1962 it took over 500 billion cigarettes to keep us happy, not counting those who roll their own, and excluding pipe tobacco, cigars, snuff, and chewing tobacco."[10] The National Center For Disease Control released a study in October of 1987 that related cigarette smoking to 315,120 deaths in our country each year. It has been said 1000 people die each day from smoking. Nonetheless Taylor states that tobacco will survive because it does fill a human need transcending all advertising clatter. The problem we may observe is that those who are using it are not surviving. It has now been scientifically established that there exists a frightening correlation between cigarette smoking and many of the degenerative diseases that are devastating people today. In particular it has been shown that there is a direct relationship of smoking to lung cancer. There is no doubt about it. We know cigarette smoking is bad news for everyone. And, as I have already noted, it is especially bad for the athlete, because it will not only bring on sickness eventually, but more immediately it will adversely affect athletic performance.

Cigarettes are a real clear and present danger, but for millions hooked on them including athletes it can be an almost impossible task to get off them. Even in light of the grim statistics concerning lighting up, however, I may report there is some good news. I have developed a program called "Smoke Breakers" which has really proved effective in programming individuals to break the dreaded habit.

Sometimes if you want to get into the water to go swimming but are afraid it's too cold, you try to ease your way in—perhaps, a little toe at a time. Sometimes it doesn't work, and you would be better off just jumping right in. Similarly, there are situations in life where you have to break a bad habit, end a bad job situation or relationship, and you try to do it little by little but that just doesn't work. In such situations it may be necessary to just make a clean break. At times it is the only way, the most effective way! We have found in a great many cases it may be the only way to stop smoking, a crash program to stop! Therefore, it is often not best to try a gradual reduction, but to just go cold turkey.

This cold turkey break when reinforced by basic supplements may be the best way to go. My program Smoke Breakers rests on the premise that *nicotine* being physically addictive must be countered with a combination of vitamins, minerals, and herbs that will liberate us from the addiction. We offer a supplement we call "Neurosed" with a carefully balanced grouping of vitamins, minerals, and herbs that are designed to control nicotine. As it is gone, it is necessary to cleanse and purify the system. This can be achieved through consumption of *fluids*. Lots of fluids will wash out the bodily system.

The cold turkey approach, the vitamin-mineral-herb supplement, and a goodly supply of fluids must be reinforced by both negative and positive conditioning. There is for one what

I HOPE THE HELL I WIN!

I call a *Life Saver Trick*, which is an accupressure technique. This involves actually pressing up on the roof of the mouth to negate the urge to smoke. Then in the SmokeBreakers program I provide a tape that produces extremely negative associations in one's mind with smoking. This is the aversive conditioning. It is necessary to get the person to feel disturbed or even sick every time the mere thought of a cigarette occurs. Listening to this tape twice a day should help build up a negative reaction to the need for smoking.

For something to be effective in the long run, or to really learn, there must be rewards as well as punishment. Thus I have the smoker use what I call PTP — positive thought process. Each and every day, ritualistically, I have the person recite his or her reason for wanting to become a nonsmoker. This may also be buttressed by *self-hypnosis*. Primarily I would have the person wanting to *overcome* the smoking habit go through a *progressive relaxation*, shedding fears and anxieties, and relaxing every cell and fiber of the body from head to toe. Then the person will emphasize planting in his or her mind positive suggestions. For the athlete the message sent to him or herself will be: You can do it without cigarettes, you will be successful!

You can see with smoking then, as with drugs or drinking, by trying to make a *gain* for your nerves or to add to your confidence or make you feel better, it is easy to become a *loser*. There are many ways one can sell one's souls to get something, but the devil, whether in the form of drugs, alcohol, or smoking is hard to please, and ends up ravaging our bodies as well.

The athlete must learn not to become dependent on anything external to improve performance, because that is a certain road to slavery. The danger may even be greater for the athlete when dealing with injuries, because they may become so disturbing that one will do anything to become healed. Here again the athlete must be extremely careful not to sell his soul for some quick fix cure. In many cases of illness today side effects of medicine may be so serious that the old joke that used to be told around Vienna in the time of Freud is quite applicable: the cure is worse than the disease. The athlete must be wary of what he or she does to attain recovery, and this then brings us to the serious problem of sports injuries.

When The Cure Is Worse Than The Disease

Sports Injuries and Sports Medicine

There are many cures floating around that end up being worse than the disease. This applies not only to home remedies, but sometimes even to *prescribed* medicines. In a most eye-opening study called *Medical Nemesis*, Ivan Illich tells us, "Medicines have always been potentially poisonous, but their unwanted side effects have increased with their power and widespread use."[1] Thus every day up to 80 percent of adults in the United States and the United Kingdom take medically prescribed chemicals. Illich points out that some take the wrong drug, some take one out of date or contaminated, and still others mix drugs into dangerous combinations. Drugs such as thalidomide and chloramphenicol which were prescribed to people were disastrous.

We certainly would not advise anyone to try to treat or cure him or herself without seeking qualified help from a medical expert, but, on the other hand, one has to be careful of any advice or medicine. A second opinion is always wise. And, where feasible, natural healing or natural healing methods will yield safer results than drugs; overloading with medication is not wise. Again, our general prescription of taking as natural and simple means as possible is often the best medicine. It also may be valuable to seek a holistic or natural oriented physician.

Athletes, of course, are particularly vulnerable to bodily injuries. Basketball playing, football, baseball, tennis, running, boxing, wrestling—whatever—the potential for hurting oneself is great. A basketball player jumps up and twists his leg when he comes down; tennis players get tennis elbow; in basketball, running or football, one is dealing with the feet; and in baseball, the shoulder.

Now, as I have emphasized, for any serious injury it is necessary to see a physician and receive proper treatment. When there is intense pain, pain that will not go away over any extended period or any infection, there should be an examination. Particularly for an athlete there will be problems, however, that require immediate treatment.

Fortunately there are some useful rules to follow to alleviate sports problems. A simple way to remember these is simply to think of the word "ICE"—apply Ice, Compression and Elevate. Compression should be used immediately. Compression keeps swelling down. Swelling can cause an injury to take a longer time to heal. Ice is also indicated. An iced compress will, as compression, reduce swelling. Ice constricts narrow broken blood vessels. This means that there will not be as much bleeding into healthy tissue. The consequence of reduced bleeding will be reduced swelling and reduced pain. Heat, of course, should not be used immediately. Heat works in the opposite manner from compression and swelling. It opens blood vessels and expands tissues. Heat increases circulation, and you would not want increased blood supply to an injury.

Having used compression and ice, *elevation* may prove quite helpful. By raising the injured part higher than the heart is a way of using gravity, and that helps drain off excess fluid.

Of course, there are other important measures which really are good common sense. Simply put, when there is pain or something hurts when exercising or performing: STOP! Further rest is essential. Any pain or injury is a way of warning us to stop, slow down or rest.

While heat *should not* be used in *initial* stages of an injury it may be a new ballgame after 48 hours. Once the injury is beginning to heal, *heat* may be introduced to the area that was hurt. In this later period, when one is recuperating, heat by increasing circulation will send needed blood to the injury. This effect can also be achieved through *massage*.

An important point to consider is that, while recuperating, a muscle not being used will atrophy and lose power. Indeed, muscles in good condition will not be capable of peak performance if not used. Gentle stretching will help in the program of rebuilding an injured athlete. One can use stretching exercises in moderation and work up to increased endurance.

Indeed, when the question of *preventing* rather than curing injuries arises, stretching must be regarded as crucially important. In medicine generally, there is new air settling, an *atmosphere* of prevention rather than *treatment*. After all, when treatment comes, it is already *too late*. The thing is to *avoid* the necessity for treatment by not becoming sick. In medicine this means to live in such a way as to keep one's immune system strong. In sports the same prescription applies. One has to keep oneself in good condition and shape so as to minimize the likelihood of getting hurt.

If prevention is the word, stretching is a top way to live by the word. Vigorous exercise shortens and tightens muscles. Such a condition renders them more vulnerable to injury. Stretching provides a much needed flexibility. Stretching reduces the incidence of sports injuries by a high percentage.

In general, I would emphasize the general approach to prevent and to recuperate from injuries. There must be a positive outlook or philosophy. Negative thinking or worrying about something going wrong can easily become a selffulfilling prophecy. Worrying something will happen may bring it on, or even subconsciously cause it. Living simply and naturally and booting one's condition with adequate rest and good nutrition constitutes miraculous medicine.

Dr. Robert Kerlan, a distinguished orthopedic surgeon now 65 years old, may be regarded as one of the founders of sports medicine. He has treated baseball luminaries such as Sandy Koufax and Don Drysdale, football star Merlin Olsen, as well as Wilt Chamberlain of basketball fame. Dr. Kerlan very much recognizes the tremendous significance of the *mind* in preventing or healing sports injuries. Kerlan is the tops as a sports physician, perhaps because he has such great empathy with athletes. It may just be due to the fact that he himself wanted very much to be an athlete.

When The Cure Is Worse Than The Disease

That great hope was smashed when he was only in his twenties, and it was discovered he suffered from what we now know to be *ankylosing spondylitis*, which causes intense pain and loss of mobility. He could not possibly be an athlete, but he could treat them. Now he sees about 1000 new patients per month in his orthopedic clinic in California.

Especially noteworthy about this fine physician is his emphasis. He says, "My whole practice is based on the idea that the mind is more important than any one of our little working parts, and I want to make sure I don't get someone depressed; that's a lot harder to cure than a knee joint or shoulder."[2]

Digby Diehl comments, "Kerlan's belief in the importance of the psyche requires him to be a psychologist as well as an orthopedist. This extra dimension is invaluable when he has to deliver bad news."[3] For an athlete to keep in shape and respond to the challenge of sports injuries, he has to think positively and relax, rest, exercise, stretch, and place great emphasis on nutrition.

The athlete has to eat for energy and defeat of fatigue, and that will help the cause against sports injuries. This means, as I have insisted upon in the chapter on nutrition, eating complex carbohydrates and cutting down on proteins and fats. I am talking about whole grains, fresh vegetables, fruit, and whole wheat pasta. Dr. Bernard Friedlander contends, "Many injury problems are food related."[4]

Ron Brown, receiver for the Los Angeles Rams and Olympic gold medalist in 1984, suffered from terrible leg cramps. He didn't think he could make it through the Olympics. Dr. Bernard Friedlander, however, came to the rescue. He got him away from junk food, and put him on generous quantities of fruits and vegetables. Added to this was a carefully chosen selection of minerals and supplements. Ron Brown thus went on a natural and nutritious diet, taking supplements and training in stretching techniques. The result was, as Martin Zucker reports, "his cramping problem had been happily reduced to an absolute minimum."[5]

Fatigue is one serious problem that is a cause of sports injuries, and one that can certainly be alleviated by nutrition. Animal protein and fats are difficult to break down. Therefore, a lot of energy is needed to digest and assimilate animal protein and fatty foods. You are buying 80 percent fat in a steak, and that is the last thing you need, particularly if you are an athlete and want maximum energy.

Athletes who feast on fast foods, and many do, invite disaster. Even when they exercise, athletes on fast food fare become overweight. Rick Mariner, trainer of the Seattle Mariners has complained that fast food eaters are more prone to tendinitis, to inflexibility and back and knee problems.

A complex carbohydrate diet can help prevent injuries, but it can also help repair injured parts. Athletes often increase protein intake to help tissue heal, but it turns out that tissue repairs on a complex carbohydrate diet. The requirement of an injury for energy is greater than for protein. Further, it has been shown that muscles must have carbohydrates. Thus when needing to rebuild muscles, the athlete must eat properly.

Particularly important for the athlete is Vitamin C because of its role in fortifying the immune system against the ravages of stress, and because of its central role in synthesizing *collagen*, the connective tissue that holds our body together. Indeed, a person afflicted with scurvy can no longer produce collagen, and the result is that his body falls apart. The cartilage and tendons weaken, the blood vessels break open, the gums ulcerate, teeth fall out, and the immune system goes.

An excellent vitamin to take along with C is P. Vitamin P is the bioflavonoid vitamin. Bioflavonoids are essential for the proper function and absorption of vitamin C. Bioflavonoids increase the strength of our capillaries. By strengthening the walls of the capillaries, they work against bruising. Dr. R.M. Woods, the team physician for the Los Angeles Dodgers, found that players using bioflavonoids lost much less playing time than players not using them. Bioflavonoids are definitely good news for athletes. It was found that football players at Louisiana State University on bioflavonoids throughout the year suffered less bruising and less hemorrhaging around sprains.[6]

There is an interesting chapter in *Eat To Win* by Robert Haas called "Heal Faster - Stay Younger: The Anti-Oxidant Story." Haas reveals that world-famous marathon champion Bill Rodgers told him, "sadly," that once an athlete passes age 30, it's all downhill. Haas insists, however, by using antioxidants an athlete can stay younger.

Tennis champ Fred Stolle used the peak performance program of Dr. Haas, and was not hindered by age. He recommends the antioxidants beta carotene, vitamin C and vitamin E. What he found was that antioxidants not only can help stave off the effects of premature aging, but they also can help to heal sports injuries faster, leaving the body stronger. Actually, aging and sports injury have a lot in common. In a biochemical sense, aging can injure and injury can age."[7] Free radicals destroy healthy tissue, including genetic material in our cells. By damaging cells, free radicals contribute to the aging process. Free radicals are cut down by antioxidants.

Diet plays an important role along with the use of antioxidants in the fight against sports injuries. The more fat one eats, particularly if unsaturated, the more free radicals one's body will produce. What that adds up to is a longer period for an injury to heal.

Along with beta carotene, ample doses of a time-release vitamin C and vitamin E, the athlete would do well to use a multivitamin and multimineral capsule to avoid any possible vitamin or mineral deficiencies that could make one more susceptible to being injured and less able to heal. At least 50mg of zinc should be taken daily. Research has established that zinc helps heal and regenerate damaged connective tissue.

Dr. Ron Lawrence, who has an excellent track record in treating athletes, recommends a regimen of vitamins and minerals to prevent and heal injury. He points out that magnesium plays a role in healing cartilage injuries of the knee, which are real occupational hazards for football players, tennis players and runners.

Athletes might try the "mega pineapple" prescription against sports injuries. The approach has been recommended by sports medicine authority Dr. Jack Kahn, a chiropractor in Florida. The prescription is to eat as much of a pineapple as you can in one hour every other day. The object is to benefit from bromelain, an enzyme contained in pineapple. Bromelain breaks down injured tissue. Dr. Kahn prescribes megadoses of B-6 along with the pineapple therapy. He puts athletes on as much as 1,800 mg. daily. B-6 functions as a "natural" diuretic and cleans one out without producing a mineral imbalance.

B-6 processes protein and makes it more available repair.

A nutrient that should have highly beneficial res athlete is CoQ10. CoQ10 is essential to the function of every single cell in the human body. It was discovered in 1957 and subsequently Dr. Karl Folkers at the University of Texas was one of the first scientists to show its basic importance in cell respiration and energy production. Since then CoQ10 has been used extensively in Japan.

It has been found that our bodies cannot fend off infection and disease without CoQ10. Supplementing our body's own capacity to supply CoQ10 with about 30 mg per day can help revitalize the immune system and help defend against infections including cancer. It can in a natural way turn back some effects of aging, can normalize high blood pressure, and, of particular importance to the athlete, it can revitalize the body and increase tolerance for exertion.

Dr. Emile G. Bliznakov and Gerald L. Hunt explain, "In each cell there are subcellular components called mitochondria. These can be likened to cylinders in the automobile engine where gasoline is ignited and explodes, resulting a force that moves the pistons..... In the human machine it is this energy that fuels the entire body."[9] What this means is that without CoQ10 our body does not get sparked, no ignition, and no production of energy.

Particularly important to our immune system are *macrophages*. Macrophages are special cells that play an essential role in fighting invaders of the immune system. Now research has shown that CoQ10 may stimulate activation of macrophages.

If one might think of CoQ10 as a kind of miracle nutrient, one may note there are researchers who think of germanium as a miracle cure. Indeed, Dr. Kazuhiko Asai, a Japanese scientist, wrote a book called *Miracle Cure: Organic Germanium*. Germanium is a trace mineral which medical researchers have found plays an essential role in the biochemistry of the body. It has been found that plants fed germanium grow at a faster rate.

Karl Loren quotes Dr. Asai as concluding, "it would be no exaggeration to call organic germanium an 'elixir' of life."[10] Research has established that plants must have germanium to allow sunlight to produce the creation of carbohydrates. This means that germanium plays an important role in the process that renews the oxygen supply of our planet, and which provides all of the food eaten on our planet.

Dr. Asai believes that on our polluted and poisoned planet we all have less oxygen than we need, and this explains why our immune system has weakened, thereby making us more susceptible to disease. In consideration of this, it is quite easy to see the value of germanium because, quite simply put, what it does is carry extra oxygen into our bodies. Of the many highly beneficial consequences of germanium one particularly important to athletes is its "energizing effect."

In his report on germanium Karl lists the following benefits:

1. It is effective against certain tumors.
2. It increases oxygen amount in the cells and tissues.
3. It decreases the sensation of pain.
4. It activates and improves the immune system.
5. It fights aging by balancing freeradical metabolism.

6. It improves stamina, endurance and enhances sex, sports performance and relieves stress.
7. In Japan it has been used in high doses to heal many serious diseases, including cancer and heart disease.

There is no doubt that in our stressful and polluted environment much benefit is to be derived from such supplements as CoQ10 and germanium along with the antioxidants; and certainly this would be all the more true for anyone, such as the athlete, who uses much energy and whose activities make him so prone to receiving injury.

A more controversial freeradical scavenger and painkiller is *dimethyl sulfoxide or DMSO*. A great deal of damage resulting from sports injuries is due to hydroxyl *free radicals*. A sports injury may see the damaged blood vessels in the injured area spilling into tissue around it, and the copper and iron in the blood causing the production of free radicals. Antioxidant vitamins can deal with these free radicals, but the advantage of DMSO is that it can be applied *externally*, directly to the location of the injury. If DMSO is applied quickly after injury it can actually eliminate bruising.

In a book on *DMSO,* from the files of Dr. Stanley Jacob and Robert Herschler, there is a chapter called "DMSO: The Athlete's Best Friend."

Daryle Lamonica, the former Oakland Raiders quarterback, testified at a Senate subcommittee hearing in July, 1980, concerning use of DMSO for injuries. He revealed that his thumb was so swollen he could not bend it. He said, "I took DMSO, there was a slight blister, but the swelling went down before my eyes. I couldn't believe it. Within five or six minutes, my skin went back to normal, and the majority of the swelling was down."[11]

Another witness was Sam Bell, the head track and field coach at Indiana University. Bell has long endorsed DMSO, having discovered it to be highly successful himself in healing an ankle injury.

Daryl Horn, a jumper at the 1964 Olympics, also had a positive experience with DMSO. Many professional football stars such as June Jones have given DMSO a very strong endorsement. Al Oerter, discus thrower and Olympic gold medalist found its use most worthwhile.

Barry Tarshis reports, "Not only are athletes high on DMSO, trainers and sports physicians like it as well."[12] Graham Reedy, team physician for the Oakland Raiders, found DMSO to have dramatic positive effects.

DMSO can produce quick and highly effective relief from acute muscular injuries because of its multiple properties. DMSO relieves the pain and inflammation that occurs in sprains, reduces swelling, relaxes muscles surrounding the injury, and may shorten the healing time for injured cells. Further, according to Dr. Jacob, DMSO is safer to use in athletic injuries than painkilling agents such as Novocain, which cause numbness. There is greater risk of aggravating an injury from the use of Novocain than DMSO. On top of this what athletes particularly like about DMSO is the speed with which it works.

Barry Tarshis reports, "The speed of the therapeutic effects of DMSO has led Dr. Marvin Paul, a member of the University of Toronto Maple Leafs, to describe it as 'the most important therapeutic agent available for the types of injuries so frequently encountered by athletes in competitive sports'".[13] Dr.

Paul even used DMSO on himself to treat a recurrent slipped disc, and announced that it worked better than anything else he ever tried.

Alberto Salazar, distance runner and winner of the 1980 New York Marathon, said that everybody uses DMSO. Another athlete enthusiastically claimed that it is tremendous for burns. There is one problem. The FDA (Food and Drug Administration) doesn't think it's tremendous and, as of 1965, made it illegal for medical uses.

DMSO is available to the public, but only for use as a "solvent." Scientists Durk Pearson and Sandy Shaw are extremely critical of the FDA's stand on DMSO as a travesty of science. I believe that DMSO has plenty of legitimate uses and that is should be available for topical use as an OTC (Over The Counter; that is, non-prescriptive) drug."[14] Of course, since DMSO is sold as a solvent it carries no instructions on how to use it medicinally, and it is impure industrial-solvent-grade and might actually contain dangerous impurities. Thus the effect of the FDA's policy is really to make DMSO available for people to use improperly. An interesting point is also brought up by Ken Sprague. He reports, "Some pro-DMSO people have charged that major drug companies don't want to see the chemical approved by the FDA because Crown Zellerbach, the big paper manufacturer, owns the patent use for it as a painkiller. A legal DMSO, say its boosters, would severely cut into sales of pain-killers already in the market."[15]

It would be difficult to disagree with the point that it would be better to make DMSO legally available for medical purposes and supervise its marketing than to follow the present policy.

While I do not know of a safe natural painkiller to substitute for DMSO, there is good news for athletes who have relied on the use of anabolic steroids. As we have seen, athletes in increasing numbers are using steroids, but these have been linked to many very serious health problems. The good news of which I speak is not that there is any safe way to use steroids, but that there may be a safe *substitute*. Recently scientists have found a natural compound that imitates the effects of anabolic steroids, one that has no harmful side effects. It is an herb, and it is quite legal. It is called *Smilax*. Steroids bombard the body with synthetic testosterone, thereby doing it damage. Smilax gently stimulates the body to naturally produce higher testosterone levels. These are safe levels and beneficial to the body. Smilax should be taken in its pure extract liquid form.

Another possibility for building muscles is the *growth hormone* GH. The growth hormone GH is released by the pituitary gland in the brain as a result of exercise, fasting and sleep among other factors. GH stimulates muscle development. Exercise at peak level releases GH, but it appears in relation to this that a little exercise is as good as nothing, for it seems any exercise less than peak output fails to release GH. It also appears that after one reaches the age of 30, exercise does not any longer result in the release of GH. Nutrients can play a significant role here. The amino acids *arginine* and *ornithine* cause GH release.

Not only does GH or growth hormone burn fat and build muscle tissue, but it is essential for tissue repair. Wounds heal because GH directs the cells in the injured tissue to repair the damage.

When The Cure Is Worse Than The Disease

GH stimulators such as arginine and ornithine should not be taken by young people still growing, as such use could result in gigantism or bone deformity. After the age of 30, however, arginine and ornithine are quite safe so long as one does not exceed the recommended dosage. Three to ten grams per day of arginine is suggested to release GH. Ornithine should be taken along with it in half the dose. The best time to take arginine and ornithine is before bed and on an empty stomach.

What becomes clear then is that what I have been advocating in this book as a natural, simple and holistic approach to sports in general is perfectly applicable in particular to sports injuries and sports medicine. Today in the field of medicine, generally, one can see the start of a revolt brewing in opposition to traditional materialistic medicine. Traditional or orthodox medicine deals with the patient as if he or she were a mechanical assemblage of parts. When a patient becomes ill, the doctor works on a part of the body that is sick. He seeks to deal with the problem by directing medicine to that part or performing surgery on it. The doctor does not deal with the patient as a whole person. Holistic medicine works on the assumption that it is not a part of the body that becomes sick but the whole person: body, mind and spirit. That is the emphasis that we are advocating in sports generally and in sports medicine particularly. For example, an athlete using an anabolic steroid is just trying to build up the muscles without regard for him or herself as a whole person with spirit and mind as well as body. In opposition to this we advocate positive thinking, spiritual development through yoga or some form of meditation, creative visualization, good nutrition and vitamin and mineral supplements.

What the athlete requires is a philosophy or an outlook that provides harmony for him or herself with the universe. The need is to put things into balance. By discovering harmony and balance the athlete will learn to achieve inner peace, and that will make possible the necessary energy for outer action.

Without learning to be a peace with himself and the world he will not be able to relax as he must. He will not even be able to rest properly, and may even experience great difficulty trying to sleep. Ironically, while athletes do not want to receive an injury that will put them on the sidelines, many athletes have great difficulty resting. They may use so much energy, get so fatigued or so worked up that they will not ever be able to get a night's sleep. And certainly sleeplessness can be a great enemy to the athlete.

Over half of our population suffer from insomnia. Each year far more than a billion sleeping pills are sold. It is sad but true, people have to go to barbiturates to go to bed. Sleeping pills do not give natural sleep. Thus one does not have a restful sleep. What usually happens then is that the person increases the amount taken. Then one develops a tolerance for the sleeping pill, and it won't work. This leads to use of different ones until the person becomes a "sleeping pill junkie."

Fortunately, as with other problems we have dealt with, there is a natural response. Reliance on drugs is unnecessary. The particular problem the athlete has, of course, is that he or she may become excessively fatigued, and that actually stimulates the brain. An athlete going to bed exhausted may be unable to sleep. Also, if there had been a great deal of excitement in a sporting event that may have the athlete too worked up to get to sleep.

When The Cure Is Worse Than The Disease

As I have said, natural remedies are the only ones. There are rules one must learn to follow. One of the worst things anyone can do is to take worries to bed. Do not eat just before going to bed. Use soft music if you find it helps.

Of particular value is the use of self-hypnosis techniques. Tell yourself your eyes are getting tired, extremely tired, very tired. Tell yourself you will soon close your eyes and sleep will come. Relax your entire body from head to toe. Feel every muscle relaxing. You many reinforce this relaxation by counting backward. Start with 100, go to 99 to 98 to 97 to 96 to 95 and so on down to falling asleep. Tell yourself when you awake in the morning you will feel wonderfully refreshed and will fell confident and good due to a peaceful night's sleep.

Now, if you cannot sleep don't fight it. That will just get you more worked up. In fact, one technique that sometimes works is that instead of trying to sleep you must try not to sleep. Sometimes trying to stay awake and concentrating on that will cause you to fall to sleep. If you really cannot get to sleep, however, do not remain in bed. Get up and do something. Then return to bed. Now you may be tired.

The technique I use is to have my clients always clear their minds before going to bed. This is effectively coupled with breathing exercises. Have a superimposed image watch a second image of yourself sleeping.

Of course, never go to bed after any strenuous exercise, nor after taking any caffeine. Never tell yourself that you are an insomniac. Don't hate the idea of going to bed for fear of not being able to sleep. Rather, think positively, and cultivate the feeling of looking forward to going to bed. If you have to think about anything, only think about nice things.

There is a nutrient that will assist in getting to sleep. It is *Valerian Root*. Research has demonstrated Valerian Root can reduce anxiety, depression, and help one sleep. What is good is that Valerian Root doesn't depress nor drug the central nervous system.

Valerian Root is more effective when used in conjunction with B-complex vitamins. B-3 or *niacin*, which is good for the nerves, and B-6 or *pyridoxine* which is calming for the nerves reinforce and amplify the effectiveness of Valerian Root. B-5 or *pantothentic acid* is valuable in reducing stress, and also well complements Valerian Root. Along with a B-complex capsule, or niacin, B-6 and B-5, magnesium provides excellent reinforcement for Valerian Root in inducing natural sleep.

Mind, Body and Spirit

To An Athlete Living To Be Old

In A.E. Houseman's poem "To An Athlete Dying Young" the sentiment is expressed that an athlete is better off to die young while still adulated than to live on in obscurity. The roar of the crowd dies down fast when an athlete's time is past. The feeling was well-expressed in the film version of Ernest Hemingway's "The Killers" with Burt Lancaster. Lancaster played the role of a prizefighter who was adored when he was winning in the big time. When he lost, however, there was a scene when cut and bruised he was abandoned to a dreary and morbid solitude in an empty and barren arena. It happens all the time to sports heroes. In Houseman's poem we read:

> And early thought the laurel grows
> It withers quicker than the rose

Thus the athlete who died young is more fortunate than

> Runners whom renown outran
> And the name died before the man

This gloomy view of the prospects of the career of the athlete is built in to a wrong conception, or we may say, wrong philosophy of sports. What we have been advocating throughout this book is the idea that in order to excel in sports it is necessary above all else to adopt a *new way of looking* at the purpose of athletics.

In the field of law, Justice Brandeis long ago realized that you cannot look at law just in terms of *legal* factors. You must introduce psychological, sociological, political, economic, and even moral data into the understanding of law. Trying to deal with legal problems purely in terms of legal data results in what has been criticized as purely mechanical or slot machine jurisprudence. One must not consider law in narrow terms if he is ever to really develop positive health, so too if one is to truly achieve peak performance in sports, he cannot conceive of sports in a narrow technical sense.

If one thinks of sports simply in narrow terms, as a competition to win, he will lose. For in doing so he will miss the benefits of playing just for the sake of enjoying the game. The mountain climber climbs the mountain just because it is there, not because he wants to *defeat* it.

We live in a very advanced technological society, and in it people have come to *worship techniques*. There is far more to being a good actor, however, than in knowing the techniques of acting. There has to be some *vital spark* that brings life to a part that could not just be written in words. The same is true in painting or musical composition or performance. What makes a painter or a musician great always goes beyond mere *technique*. A pupil can be taught the correct techniques of painting, of singing, of acting, of practicing law, but such will

To An Athlete Living To Be Old

never make one a great painter, a great singer, a great actor, nor a great lawyer. For that there must be that something extra, that quality `X', something within, perhaps *soul*.

The same applies to the athlete. The master athlete can never be simply a master of techniques. To really be a champion the great athlete must not only know the *techniques* but participate 100 percent with his full heart and soul. That is the *stuff* of which great athletes are made. That is why it must be understood that the great athlete is not performing to win, but to *play*. The great athlete is giving his or her *all* to do his or her *best*, and that is what serves his or her *interests*, not the goal of beating an opponent. The consummate athlete gives all of his or her heart and soul and mind to the performance, and that is what *electrifies* us.

What happens when anyone gets too caught up in the techniques or details is that the *purpose* for which the techniques were created becomes lost. This is the way religion petrifies. When the person gets lost in the rituals, the high ideals of religion become lost. That, of course, is precisely what the protest of Jesus against the Pharisees was all about. It is, of course, the problem of getting hung up on looking at all of the individual trees but not seeing the whole forest.

When the athlete is just trying to win or beat an opponent, the goal or purpose of sports becomes lost. Such an athlete cannot love the game for its own sake, but is just doing a job. And that is not what can ever satisfy the deepest aspirations of a full human being. Yet tragically in our post industrial world of highly developed technology, almost everything has been reduced to mechanical performance aimed at efficient results. Artistic, spiritual or moral considerations lose significance. Just doing your "job" is the thing. As industrialization advances, nature retreats. Thus one comes to live in a very artificial and plastic environment. Against this background sports have increasingly become commercialized, a professional business.

One must remember the human is not simply *homo sapiens*, or rational animal, nor is the human simply *homo faber*, man the maker or technical animal, man the worker, but the human being is also *homo ludens*, man the *player*. The human being can transcend the rules and limitations of life that bind him and tense and tighten him through *play*. Play thus is uplifting.

Father Thomas Ryan notes, "with the increasing systematization of sport, something of the pure play quality was inevitably lost. The spirit of the professional is no longer the true play-spirit; it is lacking in spontaneity, in carelessness. The transformation of sport into a commercial business pushed it further and further away from the play-spirit proper to it."[1] George Leonard remarks that we are threatened with "the gradual encroachment of professionalism with its emphasis on winning at all costs."[2] And we finally reach the point at which the famous football coach Vince Lombardi announces that "Winning isn't everything. It's the only thing."

That professional priority placed on *winning* is a killer. It causes tremendous pressure, anxiety, and stress. The athlete gets so caught up on the imperative to win that it is forgotten what the game is really about. It's as it is with the religious fanatic who gets so caught up in the *ritual* that he forgets what religion is really all about. As I have said, that was the powerful message of Jesus or Buddha or the Zen or Sufi masters: not to *blindly* follow the *letter* of the law, but to fulfill the *spirit* of it. The athlete should try to conquer himself, not his opponent. He should not try to win as such, but to always give his all and do his best. George Leonard complains that the "institutionalization of winning at all costs takes us away from the original and ultimate purpose of sports." When the athlete seeks to *win* at any cost he reduces sports to a job in big business. That idea is conveyed by the mere title of a book by college football player Gary Shaw, which in reference to the athlete is called *Meat On The Hoof*. The athlete thus instead of being a free spirit developing spiritually, mentally and physically, becomes a product to be sold, a commodity to be manipulated. Instead of experiencing sport as a beautiful art, it becomes an ugly, cut-throat business.

In this, contemporary sports are becoming like contemporary war: even when you win you lose, for the toll is so great. In the atmosphere of a violent struggle to survive, all pleasure and joy that should be central in sports becomes lost. One can see that it is in this context that the despairing fate of an athlete is such that he or she would be better off to die young. The athlete is forced to put all energy into winning, and then after winning the athlete gets burned out. Since all is focused on winning one becomes a *has been*, and is better off dead. How revealing it is that coach George Allen said "losing is a little like dying."

That is, however, only when one understands sports as a professional business, as a narrow competition. When we see sports as a means of developing ourselves, mind, body and soul, we can see they are always open to us, even as we age. Indeed, rather than *dying* after we fade out from the business of sports, sports can help us to age gracefully, to keep us in shape, and extend our lives.

I Hope the Hell I Win!

We must understand we are not in there simply to win, but to enjoy ourselves, to play, to live life more fully. Sports are not basically about competing, but about expanding our lives. If we become compulsive about *winning*, we will not have the zest and spirit to attain peak levels. And when we see sports in a fuller sense, in a bigger sense, we will not be driven to steroids or drugs to come to terms with the need for success. Then the athlete can live happily and for a long time.

George Leonard says, "Coldly scientific methods are used to coax every last centimeter or half second from the athlete, who is treated essentially as a machine. But:

> "Athletes can be given back their feelings and humanity at no long-term cost to performance. In fact, the inculcation of higher awareness may well result in break throughs in performance levels. Lifelong physical activities can be provided for every body type."[3]

Thus the new way of viewing sports must not be to get up tight trying to win, but to relax, just trying to *be*. It is the secret and works for any age. What has to be realized is that it is not mechanical building of the body to be powerful that is important in sports, but developing a mental edge and taking it easy, *relaxing*. It's beautiful and simple. Obsessively building physical power is counterproductive. The athlete taking that approach does become inflexible and wears out and is better dying young. But that's crazy.

An instructor, Jeff Kohn, is teaching some children karate. He asks a fragile eight-year-old to break a board. After five tries, it does not work. Kohn reassures him, and tells him to try later. After doing some other exercises, later on Kohn calls the eight-year-old back. He gets him to concentrate harder, but has him *relax*. This time the eight-year-old boy, Jake, *breaks the board*. The lesson ends with a meditation.

The point in the new approach to sports is not to push too hard—you can push yourself out of existence that way—but to concentrate, take it easy, and loosen up and relax. Mark Spitz, winner of seven Olympic gold medals is quoted as saying:

> If you are relaxing and subconsciously thinking about your coming race, you are going to perform at just about 100 percent efficiency.[5]

As the importance of mind over matter has come to be realized by professional sports people, a new air is beginning to appear. New things are happening. The professional football team, the Philadelphia Eagles, had a great 1980-81 season. Perhaps some of it is attributable to the fact that they used a "relaxation tank," or what we call a flotation tank. The darkened, heated water and salt solution was an ideal haven or refuge spot for our players to find peace. They could go into the tank and listen to self-hypnosis tapes or relaxing music. One player said that it was great to go in and float before a game.

When members of a professional football team get in a flotation tank and listen to selfhypnosis tapes we know we are in a new age. Athletes are increasingly coming to realize that there are philosophical, psychological and even religious factors involved in fulfilling oneself as an athlete. Rather than traditional diet, traditional brute force or traditional medicine and the used of drugs, enlightened athletes are getting into flotation tanks, meditating, visualizing.

It is reaching the point that instead of using a needle to "shoot up" drugs, athletes may take the needles of *acupuncture*. The idea of this ancient Chinese system of medicine is to heal illness by restoring balance in our lives and putting us in harmony with the rhythmic vibrations of life. This is accomplished by inserting needles into specified areas of the body to prevent any blockage that could be stopping a natural and harmonious energy flow. Basketball star Kareem Abdul-Jabbar tried it. Quarterback Roman Gabriel as well as pitcher Dave LaRoche have tried acupuncture.

Athletes to their credit are becoming open to new avenues of exploration in search of their inner as well as physical development. Some current problems, such as weight or sexual difficulties, may be approached through hypnotic age regressions. I have personally had much success employing this technique.

I have a person with a problem "visualize" in a completely white room - white ceiling, white walls, white floor. There is a calendar with the present days' date in large bold letters. The pages in the calendar start to fall. The dates fall back month by month, and then more rapidly, year by year. The further back we go, the more rapidly the pages turn. We can then stop at a predetermined time. Perhaps, the person says we should go to the fourth birthday.

Now the calendar transforms into a screen, and on the screen is a picture of the person at his fourth birthday. The person is directed to look around, and to take note of other persons around. The person must then watch himself on the TV screen. Then I have the person tell all he sees. I tell the patient I would like him to see this picture, and when it is seen raise up his right thumb. I then have him relate what is happening in the scene. The directions are: "Remain deeply relaxed, and while so remaining, relate what you are seeing." If the person sees himself as a four-year-old, he may speak as a four-year-old.

I have the person recount what is seen. After that, the direction is to change scenes. Now the person may move to school and see school chums. Then the direction is to go to age five. I have the person—in hypnotic state, of course—to raise the thumb when reaching age five, and again to tell all concerning that.

I had a woman patient who was experiencing sexual problems. She couldn't make any progress in dealing with them. I took her back in a hypnotic age regression. It turned out she had been fondled by her uncle when she was five. When we did the regression, it was of such emotional significance, she cried.

Now to relieve the person of this terrible painful memory, it wa possible to make "closure." We did that by *smokescreening;* that is I had her see the uncle. Below the screen is a switch. By means of it, the picture can be made lighter or darker. By making it darker it was possible to turn off the woman's emotional trauma.

To safely return a subject, I have them imagine being back in the white room. Then it is necessary to have the subject see calendar pages beginning to rise up and, flipping over, come back to present. Count one to five, have the subject open their eyes and remember everything vividly.

I Hope the Hell I Win!

A great deal can be unearthed concerning a person's problem or problems by returning to a forgotten source far back in the past. Now there are some who believe there are problems that didn't originate at all in this life, even at an early period. There are those who believe to really solve a disturbing problem, it is essential to go past the childhood of this life into a past life.

There are quite responsible people, such as Dr. Helen Wambach or Dr. Edith Fiore, who have arrived at the position that people have lived before and can be helped in regard to present problems by establishing contact with past lives. These doctors and other scholars have come to accept the idea that we have lived before, because, in regressing, individuals richly detailed and verifiable accounts of being in other times have popped up.

Possibly athletes may have problems that go back to another life. Exploration usually does result in illuminating revelations. One person who had a serious weight problem found that he had starved to death in his last life. Through going back to previous lives, people have learned amazing things about this present existence. Whatever one believes about the actual existence of past lives, there can be no question that past life therapy does work. It holds out the richest possibilities for giving us insight into ourselves. Many hang ups athletes have may go back to another life in another age. Thus to truly bring an athlete into full self-understanding, in order to achieve the best performance, *past life regression* may be helpful. I certainly would not advocate it in all cases or where there is resistance to it, but when there is openness to it, then it can be truly valuable.

To An Athlete Living To Be Old

I have had most positive results in doing hypnotic past life regressions with patients. The procedure, of course, is similar to an age regression. Instead of stopping at an age such as three or four, I would take a patient all the way back to the womb, and then back to another existence.

There are no limits to what we can accomplish. Not only may we go back to a past life, but we may go forward to the future. Instead of a regression there can be a *progression*. We can take someone forward and show the person as he wants to be, successful and confident. We can get the person to visualize a future script he desires, and then he will write it out in his life. We can take an athlete forward, attaining new heights he may not have dared imagine he could achieve, and he will discover that he *can do it*.

That's our story. The athlete has it within, and only has to bring it out, and it will be possible to become a master athlete. Drugs, steroids, macho posturing or pushing too hard are not necessary. The route to success is not some outer magic, but is through development of oneself.

1. Find a definite goal, which will result from the working out of a meaningful philosophy.
2. *Meditate.*
3. *Visualize.*
4. *Be Hypnotized.*
5. *Think Positively.*
6. Eat Properly—*naturally and simply.*
7. Supplement with vitamins and minerals and herbs.
8. Be open to acupuncture, dream therapy, age and even past life regressions.

Dr. Steven M. Rosenberg

9. Listen to the wisdom of your body, through such means as biofeedback or biorhythms, and practice physical exercise as taught in yoga.

You will become what you *project*, and therefore must project positive goals that you desire to realize. By thinking positively, visualizing it, dreaming creatively, and then training, you have got it made.

The athlete may daily use the autosuggestion Emil Coue taught to his students as far back as in the 1920's. The phrase has become immortal:

> Every day in every way
> I'm getting better and better.

One who can understand that will develop naturally and simply, and there will be no need to live in the *fast lane*. The athlete may *naturally* get *better* and *better* every day. There is no need to go the way of LT. In his book called *LT: Living On The Edge*, New York Giants superstar Lawrence Taylor confessed about his life in the fast lane, his selfdestructive drug habit and mistaken lifestyle. Too many athletes are living on the edge. The danger is that you can easily fall over the edge into self-torture, oblivion, or death. Living in the fast lane and on the edge, it probably is better to be an athlete dying young. To have a positive self-image of oneself as a whole person, however, it is much better to be an athlete living to be an old age while remaining eternally youthful. To be on edge, or on the edge, is self-defeating. The need is to live straight, play it straight, and get back to the center - You Can Do It! —

FOOTNOTES

GO WITH IT
LOSE YOUR MIND TO WIN YOUR GAME

1. Denis McCluggage, *The Centered Skier*, Bantam Books, 1986, p.11.
2. Sadaharu Oh and David Falkner, *A Zen Way of Baseball*, Vintage Book, Random House, 1985, p. 6.
3. W. Timothy Gallaway, *The Inner Game of Tennis*, Bantam Books, 1979, p. 1.
4. Charles A. Garfield with Hal Zina Bennett, *Peak Performance*, Warner Books, 1984, p. 27.

BE IT
MEDITATION

1. Susan Rubner and Dr, Richard Chin, *The Martial Arts*, Harper and Row, Publishers, 1978, p. 9.
2. Taisen Deshimaru, *The Zen Way to the Martial Arts*, E.P. Dutton, Inc., 1982, pg.1f.
3. Ibid. p. 1.
4. Felix Dennis and Roger Hutchinson, *The Wisdom of Bruce Lee*, Pinnacle Books, 1976, p. 7.

I HOPE THE HELL I WIN!

SEE IT
CREATIVE VISUALIZATION AND GUIDED IMAGERY

1. "The Man Who Got Inside Pelles Mind," *Philadelphia Daily News*, Wed. Nov, 1985.
2. Adelaide Bry with Marjorie Bair, *Directing the Movies of Your Mind: Visualization for Health and Insight*, Harper and Row, Publishers, 1978, p. 25.
3. Harold Sherman, *How to Picture What You Want*, A Fawcett Gold Medal Book, 1978, p. 132.
4. Ibid. p. 135.
5. Andrew Wiehl, *Creative Visualization*, Llewellyn Publications, 1958, p. 112.

FREE IT
HYPNOSIS AND SPORTS

1. See Bob Burrill, *Who's Who in Boxing*, Arlington House, 1974.
2. See Dr. David F. Tracy, *How to Use Hypnosis*, Sterling Publishing Company, 1952.
3. Sidney Petrie with Robert B. Stone, *What Modern Hypnotism Can Do For You*, A Fawcett Crest Book, 1986, pg. 121.

THINK IT
THE POWER OF POSITIVE THINKING AND SPORTS

1. Stephen La Berge, *Lucid Dreaming*, Ballantine Books, 1985, pg. 1.
2. Ibid. p.155
3. For a summary of visualization techniques adopted by athletes see Adelaide Bry, *Directing the Movies of Your*

Mind, Harper and Row, 1978, pp. 53-57.
4. Bernie Zilbergeld and Arnold A. Lazarus, "Mind Power," in *New Age*, Sept-Oct. 1987, p. 64.
5. Mark Teich and Geiselle Dodeles, "Mind Control, How to Get It, How To Use It, How To Keeo It, *OMNI*, Oct., 1987, p. 53.

THE BODY HAS ITS OWN MIND

1. W.B. Cannon, *The Wisdom of the Body*, W.W. Norton & Co., Inc. 1939.
2. Gay Gaer Luce, Body Buce, *Body Time*, Random House, 1971, p. 5.
3. Barbara O'Neil and Richard Phillips, *Biorythms: How to Live with Your Life Cycles*, New American Library, 1975.
4. Marvin karlins and Lewis M. Andrews, *Biofeedback*, Warner Paperback Library Edition, 1973, p. 24.
5. Jodi Lawrence, *Alpha Brain Waves*, Avon, 1972, p. 28f.
6. Dan Millman, *The Warrior Athlete, Body, mind and Spirit*, Stillpoint Publishing, 1979, p. 87.
7. George Leonard, *The Ultimate Athlete*, Avon, 1977, p. 63.
8. See Sophia Delza, *T'ai Chi Ch'uan, Body and Mind in Harmony*, The Good News Publishing Company.

BEYOND MCDONLDS AND DUNKIN DONUTS
NUTRITION AND SPORTS

1. See Gabe Mirkin and Marshall Hoffman, *The Sports Medicine Book*, Little Brown and Co., 1978, p.68.
2. See Dr. Robert Haas, *Eat To Win*, Signet, 1985, p.100.
3. See account in *New Frontier*, Oct. 1984.

I HOPE THE HELL I WIN!

4. "Teams Find That Minds Do Matter," by Jerry Sullivan, *The Philadelphia Inquirer*, Oct. 4, 1987 - p. 6D.
5. Idem.
6. Alice Chase, *Nutrition For Health*, lancer Books, 1954, p.233.
7. Gabe Mirkin and Marshall Hoffman, co. cit. p. 51.
8. Gary and Steven Null, *How To Get Rid of the Posions in Your Body*, Arco Publishing Company, Inc., 1977, p.75.

WHAT YOU ALWAYS TO KNOW ABOUT VITAMINS
BUT YOUR DOCTOR WAS AFRAID YOU WOULD ASK

1. Mirkin and Hoffman, op, cit. p. 50.
2. Linus Pauling. *How to Live Longer and Feel Better*, avon, 1986, p. ix.
3. Idem.
4. Leonard A. Cohen, "Diet and Cancer," *Scientific American*, November, 1987, Volume 257, Number 5, p. 42.
5. Ibid. p. 43.
6. Jane E. Brody, "Research Yields Surprises About Early Human Diets," *The New York Times*, May 15, 1979, p. C1.
7. Paavo Airola, "Are Vitamins and Minerals Really Necessary," *The Health Quarterly*, July-August, 1982, p. 28. (article was reprinted with permission from *The Holistic Health Lifebook*, complied by Berkely Holisitc Health Center, 1980).
8. Neva Jensen, "Nutrition and the Athlete," *The Herbalist*, July, 1980, p. 53.
9. Frances Sheridan Goulart, "Herbs for Endurance," *The Herbalist* July, 1980, p. 53.
10. Betty Kamen, "Chicken Soup - and Other Adaptogens," *Let's Live*, October, 1987, p. 56.
11. Frances Sheriden Goulart, op. cit. p. 53.

_____ FOOTNOTES

12. Susan Smith Jones, "Exercising With Help From the Bees," *The Herbalist*, July, 1980, p. 52.
13. Carlson Wade, "Super Energy in a Tiny Capsule," *Your Good Health Renew and Digest*, Vol. 1, No. 2.
14. Richard Passwater, "Octacsosanol," *The Health Quarterly*, Oct. 1982, p. 14.
15. See *Vitamin B-15* (Pangamic Acid) Russian Publication by V/O medexport, Moscow, U.S.S.R., 1968 with a foreword by the Co-Discover Ernst T. Krebs, Jr.

LOSING TO WIN
THE NEED TO WIN OVER YOUR OWN NEEDS

1. Gabe Mirkin and Marshall Hoffman. *The Sports Medicine Book*, Little Brown and Co., 1978, p. 84.
2. See Nicholas Pileggi, "There's No Business Like Drug Business," *New York*, Dec. 13, 1982.
3. See David Groves, "The Rambo Drug," *American Health*, Septmeber, 1987.
4. See Ibid. P. 46.
5. See Pat Croce, "The Dangers of Steroid Use," *The Philadelphia Inquirer*, Oct. 25, 1987, p. 4-I.
6. Idem.
7. Ken Sprague, *The Athlete's Body*, L.P. Tarcher, inc. 1981. p. 190.
8. Katherine Ketcham and L. Ann Mueller, M.D. *Eating Right To Live Sober*, New American Library, 1983, p. 54.
9. Norman Taylor, *Narcotics*, A Delta Book, New York, 1963, p. 119.
10. Ibid. p. 120.

I Hope the Hell I Win!

WHEN THE CURE IS WORSE THAN THE DISEASE
Sports Injuries and Sports Medicine

1. Ivan Illich, *Medical Nemesis*, Random House, 1976, p/ 27.
2. Digby Diehl, "Not For Athletes Only," *Modern Maturity*, Oct.-Nov., 1987, p. 26.
3. Idem.
4. Quoted in Martin Zucker, "Athletic Injuries," *Let's Live*, Feb, 1987. p. 10.
5. Idem.
6. Ibid. p. 12.
7. Dr. Robert Haas, *Eat To Win*, New American Library, 1983, p. 131.
8. See martin Zicker, op. cit, p. 12f.
9. Emile G. Bliznakov and Gerald l. hunt, *The Miracle Nutrient Coenzyme* Q10, Bantam Books, 1987, p. 9.
10. Karl Loren, *The Report on Germanium*, Life Extension Educational Service, 1987, p. 13.
11. Barry Tarshis from the exclusive files of Dr. Stanley Jacob.

Author Contact

Please feel free to write for information on the services provided by Dr. Rosenberg. A free stress kit will be included with your request.

Send a S.A.S.E. to:
Dr. Steven M. Rosenberg
8080 Old York Rd. (#206)
Elkins PK., PA 19027